THE PLANT-BASED RUNNER

A PERSONAL GUIDE TO RUNNING, HEALTHY EATING, AND DISCOVERING A NEW YOU

D0967795

JONATHAN CAIRNS

The Plant-Based Runner: A Personal Guide to Running, Healthy Eating, and Discovering a New You

Publishing services provided by  Archangel Ink

ISBN-13: 978-1-7291-7020-5

If a man writes a book, let him set down only what he knows.
I have guesses enough of my own.

Johann Wolfgang von Goethe, writer and statesman

YOUR FREE RESOURCE GUIDE TO
MY TOP 5 MARATHONS

Before you begin reading, I have a free bonus for you!

In addition to the information already provided in this book, I've created a resource guide for my top 5 marathons.

To receive your free guide, sign up for my mailing list by visiting jcruns.com.

By signing up, you'll also be one of the first to know of any pending book releases or updated content, and be first in line for exclusive deals and future book giveaways.

Immediately after signing up, you'll be sent an email with access to the bonus (if you don't see it in your inbox, check your spam folder).

Thanks so much, and enjoy!

–Jonathan

GRATITUDE

This book began over a glass of wine, as some of my most inspired moments have. This time I was sitting in the sun, on holidays in the south of Spain. I don't know if it was the sun, the wine, the holiday or the combination of all three, but whatever the reason, I was relaxed and open to the possibilities. Writing a book about getting fit in your fifties seemed doable. (Fit from 50 was the working title for a long time). That was over three years ago.

As a first time writer, I took all the help I could find.

I did a lot of Googling on how to publish a book and a few tips I took on board really helped the manuscript take shape. The first tip was to take on a group of beta readers. These are kind souls who are enlisted when you have a manuscript that resembles something like a book and are asked to give an honest, constructive, critique of the content with the aim of helping you get closer to the final draft. I'm not sure I would have raised my hand to the task of reading the thoughts of a novice writer. To those who said yes, and gave me feedback, I sincerely thank you—Dan Keogh, Joanne Finn, Dylan Macaulay, Karl Troy, Shannon Stevenson, Bernard Hyde, Peter Cahill, Heidi Herman, Douglas Cameron, Edel Kennedy, Tim Boland, Niall Barrett, Sharon Ohara, Rachel Wilson, Carmel Winters, Andrew O'Reagan.

Thanks to Neil Fitzgibbon for being there. Jordan Ring and Kristie Lynn for your support at Archangel Ink.

To everyone who put on their running shoes and has run beside me, I hope you got as much from it as I did. Thank you.

I have a huge circle of friends and family who loved me (regardless of my weight or fitness level) that made me the kind of person who—along with the help of a glass of wine—thought maybe I had a story that would resonate with others and be worth exploring. I come from a family of ten. My mum and dad, along with my three brothers and four sisters who have all gone on to have families of their own too; so I will be forgiven if I don't name check them all. To the Cairns crew, thank you for always laughing, always supporting and always knowing when to make me the butt of the joke.

Finally, thanks to Fiona for marrying me. Jem, Chris and Shay, having you in my life makes me want to be the best dad I can be.

CONTENTS

PROLOGUE

The miles passed slowly, and darkness came. Around Mile 30, I could feel my body struggling. The woods became eerie. Had zombies appeared, they wouldn't have been out of place. *Best to keep moving,* I thought.

On hour ten, Mile 40, I was in trouble. I was falling apart. All the positive quotes and sayings I had written down counted for nothing now. I was past it. My legs hurt, my lungs were contracting, and I had difficulty catching a full breath. My kidneys hurt. It was all pain now. Resistance was futile.

I had become one of the zombies.

Dropping in the woods held no fear for me now. Before the race, I had asked Fiona to make sure I started the next lap if I wanted to quit. Being timed out and disqualified is very different to giving up.

As I lay over a table trying to convince my body to get back up, my wife, Fiona, said, "You know you're going back out."

I said, "No, I am not. I can't."

"Yes, you are," she said.

"I don't think I can stand without throwing up."

"Whatever. You're still going back out," she said.

At the start line, I couldn't stand without holding on. I had to keep moving. Forwards, sideways, just to stay upright. About a third of the way around the loop, there is a waterfall with a bank and a drop of about eight or ten feet. I thought if I fell in, I would do some damage but probably live. I decided to "accidentally" fall in when I got there.

1

In total darkness with only the narrow beam of light attached to my forehead, I missed it. After the race, Fiona said she hadn't been sure I would make it back from that loop.

Running alone in the woods, in the dark, in pain, is an experience. My thoughts flowed and jumped unchecked. My energy tanks were empty. My sane mind left me, and my demons moved in. Two laps later, I finished the loop 2 minutes and 30 seconds late. At 3 minutes past midnight, 12 hours, 2 minutes, and 30 seconds in, and 50.4 miles from the starting point, I was disqualified.

My night was over.

INTRODUCTION

Believe nothing, no matter where you read it,
or who said it, even if I have said it,
unless it agrees with your own reason
and your own common sense.

Buddha

Disclaimer: running can kill you. It can cause a multitude of injuries. If you act on any information in this book, you may suffer death or injury. You may also lose weight and look and feel fabulous, inside and out. Checking yourself out with your medical practitioner is a good move if you're over forty, or if it's been a while since you (ahem) moved regularly—whether you act on this book or not.

This book is about how to get slim and strong. It's about how I got fit and healthy. It explores my journey from struggling to run around the block to completing the Belfast to Dublin 107-mile race. It contains my motivation, my methods, and my story—down to my meals, my snacks, my thoughts, and my training. It happened one step and one bite at a time.

Being active is now part of my identity. But it wasn't always that way. I'm grateful for having the health to walk, run, cycle, swim, dance, and jump up and down if I feel like it. I'm grateful for what exercise and healthy eating have done for me and for how they make me feel. Right now, you are what you ate, and if you don't make time for wellness you need to make time for sickness. I'm not a dietician, but everything you're about to read has been tried and tested over and over by me.

Being healthy is as much about how you think as how you act. All the evidence points in the direction that regular exercise makes you live longer and improves your quality of life. This book will tell you the story of how that happened in my life and will offer you a roadmap to begin making changes in your life. The first steps are the hardest. I will help you navigate.

So you've decided you're not happy with your place in this life right now. You thought about changing, and bought this book. What happens next? This next step is different for everyone, and it's the step that most find the hardest. I call it the Nike Step.

Just do it.

So why don't we?

I have a party on Friday, so I'll start the new me on Monday.

Well, I'm meeting Jenny from the book club on Wednesday, so maybe I'll start on Thursday.

Payday is two weeks away. Maybe if I wait, I could get myself some training gear first.

Actually, I should look into getting a gym membership when I get paid.

I think Tom said he was thinking of going jogging at the weekend. I'll wait and see if we could go together.

We have so many excuses, so many things we think we need to do first. Meanwhile …

Summer becomes winter. Young becomes old. Health becomes sickness. Life becomes death.

Procrastination is a human design flaw, not a personal failing. We need to be aware of it, understand it, and deal with it.

There is a way to do this. Today, **no matter what**, put on your runners, put one foot in front of the other, and go for a thirty-minute run. If you walk most or all of the way, it doesn't matter. You have gotten off your gluteus maximus and started on the physical journey to wellness. As long as you push yourself to the point of sweating, your journey has begun!

Cool gear, gym memberships, training partners—they can all wait another day.

How I Got Started

When I awoke the day after my fiftieth birthday, instead of walking to the fridge I started to jog. I found everywhere I normally walked or shuffled to I was now jogging. Before long I was running marathons. *Voila!*

Of course, that's not how it happened. In my mid-forties I started to lose sight of myself. I was in a miserable relationship. I hadn't time for exercise and was always too busy doing something "very important." I spent a lot of time travelling between the United States and Ireland, and I spent countless hours on flights, in airports, hotels, and restaurants. My idea of a good healthy meal was a late-night bottle of wine and a big steak. I put on a few stone without noticing. One afternoon I was in New York City crossing a road, and I misjudged the speed of the oncoming traffic. I had to sprint to get off the road. My left calf muscle, unfamiliar with sudden movement, got a shooting pain as my muscle tore. I used to play rugby—now I was falling apart crossing the road!

Like a lot of people who lose shape and fitness, I hadn't noticed. I was mid-forties and in the worst shape of my life. Knowing that you are a few stone overweight and totally unfit is a good thing. Knowing how to rectify it is another.

Because I'm Worth It

I'm now aware that the road to a happy, healthy, strong, fit me is taken day by day, bite by bite, thought by thought. It's a series of choices, decisions, and habits.

For me it starts before I go to bed. If I have my food prepared the night before, I am cutting out the chances of making poor decisions the next day. Every meal, every snack, every drink is an opportunity to pick something that will boost or repress my health. I find when I'm better prepared, it's easier to make healthier choices.

Discipline is huge, and I can't apply it to some things and not others. So I start the day by getting up with the alarm. No snooze button. It's important to me that I control my day and not let it control me. I will have my running or training gear clean and ready, so when I get in from work, I know what I'm doing.

If you're like most people, you think you read everything with an open mind and form your views and opinions based on your accumulated knowledge. But the truth is, most of us don't. We have set views, and we seek out information that reinforces our mind-set—it's called confirmation bias. *Confirmation bias* is the tendency to seek out information that confirms one's pre-existing beliefs or, the "I knew I was right" mind-set. I ask you to be as open-minded as you can as you read the following pages.

What I have learnt, I share with you in this book. Hopefully it's easy to read and set out in steps that you can follow. It even contains the recipes of my daily eating habits and the training I use to stay strong. As the opening pages note, I have put nothing in this book that I do not know to be true.

Interspersed throughout the book are accounts of several marathons I have run in the last few years. Marathons aren't for everyone, you should set your own fitness goals. I have included these anecdotes to show that there are no limits to what you can do once you think healthy and start moving. I'm often asked, "Why do you run so much?" The answer is easy: "Cause I'm worth it."

Sometimes in our busy thirties and forties we can lose sight of ourselves, certainly our health. Maybe family life, work, or our parents' example gives us reason to justify our poor choices. Maybe we find it's physically harder to build muscle now that we produce very little testosterone. Or maybe we just use age as a cover for laziness. It doesn't really matter.

What matters now is what we do today.

I changed my life one step and one bite at a time. I used running. You might use rowing, cycling, dancing, weight lifting, or walking. If it works for you, take it and own it. Someday we're all going to die. All we can do is improve our living time.

You don't have to be sick to get healthy.

If you still need a reason to read this book, take a look at the following page.

35 REASONS WHY YOU SHOULD READ THIS BOOK

1. You are sick of being fat.
2. You want to be fit.
3. Your life is shit.
4. You are tired of being invisible.
5. You want better sex.
6. You are approaching fifty and want to make the most of your life.
7. You feel the best of your living years are over.
8. You feel young but look old.
9. You want to feel hot, again.
10. You need somewhere to channel your pain.
11. You want to run.
12. You want to be the best version of you.
13. You realise you will be dead for a very long time.
14. You want to like yourself.
15. You like reading books about running.
16. You are interested in nutrition.
17. You want to be a skinny bitch.
18. You know the author.
19. You like the cover.
20. You want to train for a mini marathon, marathon, or ultra.
21. You don't want to feel so sad.
22. You are ready to take responsibility.
23. You are afraid of the dark.

24. You are suffering.

25. You are diabetic.

26. You are pissed off with your parents.

27. You are angry at the cards you have been dealt.

28. You love yourself.

29. You want to love yourself.

30. You want to be proud of yourself.

31. You want to set an example to your kids.

32. You are ready.

33. You want to be present and in control.

34. Your life needs a positive change of direction.

35. _____.

(Fill in ...)

MY JOURNEY

How I Got Moving

Starting out on a healthy path was hard for me, but it quickly became empowering and exciting. Like anything, once I gained momentum, powerful changes entered my life one after another. As I got fitter, my eating habits started to change. I found certain foods didn't support my running goals. Drinking alcohol didn't either. I stopped eating so much meat and gravitated towards less heavy foods. I found that even three days after eating meat I would get a stitch when exercising. My running habit made so many of my other habits fall in line.

Find your comfort zone. Then leave it.

Regrets in this life are inevitable, and I have plenty. Like anyone who lives to fifty, I carry baggage. My coping mechanism is to remain fit. The reason I started running is always with me; I can't outrun it. I have tried. My separation from my ex-partner, while good in itself, had resulted in me not seeing my eldest daughter for several years. Running with a knife in your gut hurts. But not running with a knife in your gut hurts too.

Following my separation, I spent the first of many years in and out of court monthly, even weekly, to try and increase access to my children. For the most part, these efforts were unsuccessful. About three years after my separation, a judge pointed out that "unlike most separated couples," our relationship continued to deteriorate. I was well aware of this. My ex and I hadn't managed a conversation in two years. We have three children together; you can imagine our lack of communication created a disastrous outcome.

One evening I came out of the family court enraged by the pain of injustice and bound by a feeling of total impotence. I was seeking more access, and once again I left court with less. I couldn't speak. I threw off my suit, changed into my running gear, and headed up the mountain. I'm not a crier, but that day I couldn't stop crying. I struggled, sweated, huffed, puffed, and cried. At one point I screamed until I had no screams left.

Some wounds can't be healed, but I found that being fit and healthy makes me stronger; it helps me to keep the tinted glasses off and look at life straight. When fit, I'm more able to face everything with accountability, responsibility, and hope. Physical fitness gives me a feeling of well-being that I never knew existed. A sort of control. I can look at my old self and say, "Look at me. I'm the captain of the ship now."

Running is a strange activity. While it attracts a lot of competitive people, it mainly attracts a different kind of competitive person— the kind who competes with himself, as opposed to competing with others. Competing on the inside as well as the outside.

Just over a year after my separation, I started going out with Fiona. We both had a strong interest in finding out about health, food, and exercise. Fiona's dad died of cancer way too young, and she's always had a desire to learn to live and eat healthier. Like me, she doesn't take herself too seriously. Five years later, we married.

Learning Proper Nutrition

One day I came across a book, Jason Vale's *The Juice Master's Ultimate Fast Food*. I read a lot of books—often more than one at a time. I'm usually working my way through one fiction and one non-fiction simultaneously. But this book? I could not put it down. I was totally taken by it. It advises readers on ways to feel and look better that don't just involve exercise. Vale's approach taught me the truth in the phrase "You are what you eat."

Fiona had bought a juicer years before we met, but it had just been gathering dust. We cleaned it off and decided to make juicing vegetables a daily activity in our house. I've since switched to making smoothies in a blender. I switched for two main reasons:

1. I like eating the whole food (the juicer extracts the juice, and the fibre is waste).

2. Smoothies are quicker to make and require less clean-up.

A next natural step along my running journey was to start reading everything I could get my hands on in relation to running, fitness, and nutrition. Several books had a strong influence on me; I still turn to them regularly. In particular, *The China Study* by T. Colin Campbell and *Clean* by Alejandro Junger, opened my eyes to a new way of looking at my health and the power I had at every meal.

My children are vegetarians, which helped me. Cooking vegetarian food for them during their growing up years meant I was familiar with what was needed to replace a piece of meat. It certainly made the early days of eating no meat easier.

All the changes in my diet have happened organically and over time. If I had started by giving up sugar, meat, and dairy, I would have gone hungry and maybe insane. Ten years on and I'm aware that everything I eat is either making me stronger or poisoning me. If it's the latter, it doesn't always stop me, but I'm conscious of what I'm eating and drinking, and I do it in the knowledge that I'm responsible for my own health. My life is totally in my hands. Knowledge is my power.

When it comes to justifying eating all the crap around you, I often hear people say, "Life's too short." That can be a bit of a self-fulfilling prophecy. I suppose it comes back to taking responsibility for yourself. Every meal is a choice. I make better choices for myself now—several times a day, every day.

Every time you eat or drink
you are either feeding disease or fighting it.

Heather Morgan

If you embark on this road, you'll need a thicker skin to go with your new lifestyle. People feel like they have the right to comment on what you choose to eat. For some reason, it's frowned upon to comment when your obese colleague has a can of coke and a bag of crisps with their lunch, but it's okay for them to ask what's the point in eating a curry if there's no chicken in it. It continues to surprise me how many people think that what they choose to eat is *normal* while everything else is odd and perfect fodder for a whole host of probing comments and questions like:

1. Why don't you eat meat? You used to love bacon.

2. Have a little slice of cake. Ah, you have to have some. There's no pleasure in life without dessert.

3. What did you have for your breakfast / lunch / dinner?

4. But if you're coming over for lunch, what will you eat?

5. Is there anything you can order in that restaurant?

6. Would you bring something for yourself to eat? I wouldn't know what to cook you.

7. You're no fun anymore.

8. Really? No meat? Not even chicken?

9. Oh, there's just a little sugar in it. You wouldn't even taste it.

10. No, we won't come over for Christmas dinner. What would we eat if there were no turkey and ham?

I just do not hang around anybody that I don't want to be with.
Period.
For me, that's been a blessing and I can stay positive.
I hang around people who are happy, who are growing,
who want to learn, who don't mind saying sorry or thank you.

John Assaraf, author

I am a coeliac, so I have digestive issues with a lot of foods. You may be interested to know I have found a lot of people who are not coeliac have just as many digestive issues as myself. And they don't necessarily know it. These are the rules I try to live by:

1. Food needs to rot quickly. Any foods that take long periods to go off tend to be bad. Have you seen the McDonald's burger from 1996?

2. Food needs to pass through you quickly. Like fruit and vegetables. The three-day cycle of meat is out. The faster food goes through you the faster you absorb the nutrients and the less fermented rotten foods you have to deal with. The faster food is digested the better it is on your digestive system.

3. Along with your food, hydration is essential to a runner. When the blood is properly hydrated it will be thinner, enabling its efficient distribution throughout the body. This will slow your heart rate and certainly make running less painful/more enjoyable.

4. White is shite. Throw out everything white (rice, pasta, bread), and replace it with brown.

5. I always pick organic if I can afford it.

You have to believe in yourself when no one else does—
that makes you a winner right there.

Venus Williams

What I do is a bit extreme for a lot of people. I get that. Most people are not training for distance running and do not require maximum efficiency from their bodies. For most, cutting back on sugar, processed food, and animal products will make a big difference in their lives. Add in regular exercise and you will be on a sustainable healthy path.

Recently, I was running with my brother Caleb in West Cork along Sheep's Head. It's a beautiful peninsula that juts out of Southern Ireland between Mizen Head and the Beara Peninsula like three toes. On this trail run, with sea on both sides, we were looking down at Whiddy Island off Bantry when Caleb said to me, "What if everything you know is wrong?" I laughed. It's never a bad time to be reminded not to take life too seriously.

A Message to My Younger Self

I found it incredibly hard to make it past the first few months of my running habit. And for good reason—it's incredibly hard. And giving up is easy. A lot of the time I felt like a half-dead fish swimming upstream. Excuses flowed freely.

I have a bad knee.
I don't like running.
I'm too busy.
The kids are too young.

But, run by run, meal by meal, decision by decision, I started to become the "me" I wanted to be. That "me" has long since been and gone. My vision of myself shifts all the time now as I achieve my goals and set new ones.

If I were to go back in time to the year 2007 and meet myself, I would have a lot to say. I would start with something like this: "Yo, J, the key to the next ten years is *discipline*. Move your body. Run, walk, swim, or go to the gym. Aim high. Be consistent, and never, ever give up. You will lose stones and become unrecognisable to yourself. You will learn to wake up feeling fabulous. Life is out there, and it's so worth it."

I would have thought the future me was on drugs.

If you can't solve a problem,
it's because you're playing by the rules.

Paul Arden

There is comfort, relief, and power in movement. There can also be pain, but I don't think it ever overshadows the joy of movement. Walking around the block used to be an achievement. Now running a 100km race carries the same weight. The first step is the hardest. The first week takes your all, and then some. The first month can be just as tough mentally as it is physically.

Friends started to say, "Are you still on that healthy buzz?" Convincing myself that I was physically and mentally made to feel good every day was one of my hardest hurdles. There is no path. No sign says, "This way."

Having the good thoughts was the first port of call.

Taking "action" was the second.

Building the bridge between the two took time, care, and effort.

Looking back, that was hard; what followed was relentless. Making myself "act" three times a week took all the mental and physical strength I could muster. When there is no light at the end of the tunnel, there is only discipline, belief, and action.

Calling Myself a Runner

Many months later, at the beginning of a road race, I heard an announcement: "Would all runners please head for the start line." Being called a runner made me feel like a bit of an impostor at first. Eventually, and without noticing, the label started to fit.

I used to keep the following stuck to my fridge:

- What do I have to think to get to where I want to go?
- Schedule is how we manifest our intentions to the world.
- What do I have to do today to get me one step closer to where I need to be?

What about you? Where are you on your journey to improved health? No matter where you are—beginning, end, or somewhere in the middle—don't give up. Find a source of motivation and stick it on your fridge. Get it in front of your face and inside your mind. One day at a time: don't give up.

I still devour every book I can get on training, running, and nutrition. Books that have inspired me are listed in the appendix at the end of the book. What are you reading to fuel your growth? What actions are you taking to light the next leg of your journey?

Act as if what you do makes a difference. It does.

William James

DON'T BLAME
THE HOLIDAYS

YOU WERE
FAT IN AUGUST

ROME MARATHON, ITALY, 21ST MARCH 2010 (MY 1ST MARATHON)

I had no idea how unprepared I was that day I stood in the shadow of the Colosseum, waiting for the starting gun. Fiona and I had prepared as best we could, with only one minor hiccup. I had rehearsed the early morning routine a few times. Up 3 hours before race time to eat a bowl of porridge with a small bit of milk and drink a glass of warm water. That was my routine. What could go wrong?

I took the porridge out of my suitcase and added milk from the fridge…then I noticed the milk was lumpy and had gone bad. I had no more porridge or food. Being coeliac, I had brought all my food with me to Rome. Just before panic set in, I found a half-eaten bagel from the flight in my jacket pocket. Saved.

Everything else went to plan, our train to the starting line was on time, and we had packed the amount of gels required to fuel the 26.2 miles. I don't use gels or drink milk now. I find sugary gels give me an immediate boost but drop my energy levels shortly afterwards. And I know from experience that any form of dairy interferes with my breathing. I talk more about sugar and dairy in the "Fuel" chapter.

Moments before the starting gun, Fiona noticed my shorts were inside out. I took it as a reminder not to take myself too seriously. We had barely enough time to laugh then we were off.

The first five miles we were giddy with excitement and overwhelmed by the number of runners. About 20,000. The second five miles were not so easy. The endlessness of a marathon started hitting home. Feelings of despair and questions along the line of *What was I thinking?* flooded in. Miles 10 to 15 were a struggle. Every five miles

I took a gel for an energy boost. I sipped water and walked through every water station, which was about every three miles. The plan was simple: Slow jog start to finish. With a big chunk of luck, nothing would stop us from finishing. How hard could it be?

What I overlooked was that I had skipped most of my long runs. Instead of running four or five times a week, I ran two or three. When I didn't feel like running more than a few miles, I didn't. Inexperience and laziness had won me over. When presented with a choice, I had taken the easy option in training. I wasn't aware that all the work for a marathon is done in advance. There is no reward without the work. None.

At Mile 16 there was a loudspeaker blasting out "Heroes" by David Bowie. Sometimes it's the small things you hang onto. I remember the boost I got from hearing a song I like. It was as if they were playing it just for me. We plodded along, and the crowds and noise kept my legs going. I didn't notice the miles passing from Miles 15 to 20. Maybe I did, and I just can't remember. They say running is a bit like childbirth: it gives you amnesia. The occasion and the realization that I was actually running a marathon made everything feel surreal.

At Mile 20 we entered St. Peter's Square, Vatican City. There was a sharp turn and some runners, confused and short of oxygen to the brain maybe, turned too sharply and started running back the way we came. It was funny, but I was only a few breaths away from doing the same. Now it was about not stopping; I knew if I stopped, I wouldn't start up again. My legs, feet, and lungs hurt. We were now heading for the Colosseum and the finish line.

I tried not to think of the history. The thousands of men slaughtered here for the amusement of the Romans. It seemed a bit ironic that we were racing *to* the Colosseum and not away from it. Crossing the finish line, I was astounded to see so many people behind us.

First chance, I rang my kids back home in Ireland. My youngest, who was five at the time, picked up.

"I finished the marathon," I said, bursting with excitement and emotion.

"Did you win?" she replied.

"No," I said.

"So what are you ringing me for?"

I didn't really have an answer to that. Trust kids to put your feet back on the ground.

We wore our medals for three days and had to hire mopeds to get around Rome as we couldn't walk properly, but it didn't matter—we'd finished. Every marathon runner we met the following days treated us and each other as heroes. Just to be part of the finisher's club was special. We were all on our own journey, and it felt very satisfying.

The occasion was only the last few hours of a four-month adventure. I saw thousands of very healthy-looking people. You don't see many overweight people in a marathon. When the race was over, there was a buzz, and runners talked about where they had run and were going to run next. I felt a strong healthy energy. There was clearly a bigger picture here.

I was starting to realise that it's not the race that matters—it's the lifestyle. I was on a high for a long time and wanted it to continue. Now every time I run I try and remember to appreciate that I'm strong enough and well enough to run. To focus on the journey is important because now I have been injured enough times to know that if my thoughts are on the next event only, I can be setting myself up for a big fall.

If you realised how powerful your thoughts are,
you would never think a negative thought.

Peace Pilgrim

MOTIVATION

*What if, on your last day on earth, the person you have become
could meet the person you could have become?*

There is immense satisfaction in setting a target, working incredibly
hard, and achieving it. Over the last decade I have learnt to take
responsibility for myself. That's 100% responsibility 100% of the time.
My life and health are no one's fault but my own.

There is only one journey, going inside yourself.

Rainer Maria Rilke, poet and novelist

Make One Right Choice at a Time

Without motivation there is no reason to get out of bed. Every day we
face a multitude of choices. It takes discipline and constant training
to make the ones that are best for us. When I started jogging, I
used to spend some time going over all the daily crap in my head. I
questioned every decision.

Did it benefit my family?
Did it benefit me?
Will it benefit either in the future?

Every day from the time you open your eyes, you are faced with
choices. Like me, you need to learn to make the ones that work
for you, and keep making them, every day. With practice, you start
making more right decisions for you, for your health.

Here are two options to begin my day:

A) Monday morning and I'm wide awake, waiting the 4 minutes
before the alarm goes off. I wait, not sure why. I am organised and

ready for the week, I feel fabulous. The prospect of another week and the good and the bad that it may bring gives me butterflies in my stomach. I sit up with the alarm, glance at my stomach, and have a moment's satisfaction thinking of the jumbo tyre I used to carry. I head for the shower and try not to sing en route. I'm still a crap singer.

B) Monday morning and I'm feeling like I just closed my eyes 10 minutes ago. The alarm is too damn loud. I feel sluggish, fat, grumpy, and bloated. As I walk to the shower, my throat reminds me I'm dehydrated. It's hard to see past the morning. My head feels heavy.

This was my choice. I chose A. Sometimes, but rarely, I wake in B. Most of the time I wake in A.

Only action counts.

Know Your Motivation

Move the day forward, and I leave work tired, I arrive home tired. It's dark outside and cold, maybe raining. I'm hungry. I think I should go for a run. This is the moment motivation counts for everything.

Right now you need to know what your motivation is, and it better be good, or else you're not moving off the sofa.

With me it was my children. Being a "separated dad," I was suffering from seeing my kids only every second weekend. I needed to counter that. I was also unfit and too heavy. I needed every moment with my kids to count. I wanted to run around with them. They loved football, hurling, rugby, Frisbee, any outside activity, with or without a ball. Like most children, they had unlimited energy. I didn't want to be watching them from the window.

Tired and cold, heading out into a wet night, I knew the why; the how looked after itself. Initially anyway. I run for different reasons now.

To change the direction of your life is not easy. It's hard, and takes time and support. Whatever your reasons for wanting to get healthy, you're probably going to need support. To have your partner (or friends) on board, will be huge. Without Fiona, I would never have made it. Initially, it felt like I was swimming uphill, against the tide. If I were to do it again I would give myself clear goals and more medium-term targets to achieve en route. That way, I wouldn't have expected instant results and might not have beaten myself up so much.

I looked outside for inspiration too, wherever I could find it. I joined National Black Marathon Association, an American running group on Facebook, as part of my plan to draw strength from every source possible. They published great motivational posts every day, along with stories of ordinary runners starting out. It was safe, and I could remain anonymous. Because no one knew me, no one was going to say, "What? You're not a runner." There was more chance someone might say, "Hey, you're not black." (As it turned out, nobody said that either.)

I used to run with a woman who one day said, "I love the morning after our runs most of all. I feel like a skinny bitch." Skinny or not, she knew the why. Also, on the day following her feel-like-a-skinny-bitch runs, she made better choices. We ran on a Wednesday night, and she said she always ate the healthiest meals on Thursdays. Her self-esteem was highest on those days after our runs. It's no coincidence that she ate best on Thursdays. She felt worth it.

Find a Rhythm of Discipline

Even with clear motivation it can be hard to hold it to the forefront every day. Some mornings it's just so cold and dark outside of the bed. That's when habit and discipline take over.

Deciding to get fit and into shape is probably the first large step. Doing it is the second. There is a bit in between, and I know it sounds easy when you read it, but it all comes down to discipline. Without discipline your change will not come. Your inner fat self will win again and again.

Think hard and decide on the *why*. You may not know it yet, but you are going into battle with yourself, and possibly those around you. Your *why* needs to be crystal clear.

Hard work works. Plan your year with goals in mind. Your month, your week, and your day. If you're going to be one of the few who stands up, you've got to be the one that stands up prepared for war.

I have heard it said that a lot of people never start because they don't want to be seen starting at the bottom. You can't buy better health and fitness; you have to make it. The good news is, I can show you how.

Don't allow anyone to project their fears onto you.

It is not all about running. Running isn't for everyone. Running never appealed to me, in any format. Running is hard. But what is harder is being a runner and overweight and unhealthy. They just don't go together. Like oil and water. Start running, and be prepared to be a slimmer, more gorgeous you. Sounds awful, doesn't it?

Even if you are a runner or are planning to be a runner, marathons may not be your thing. The challenge never appealed to me. A race of 26.2 miles is ridiculous. It really should have been shortened to 25 or 23, or maybe 10, but it wasn't. The key to running a marathon is well known: train for an appropriate amount of time with a sufficient number of long runs. There are plenty of training programmes online to choose from. I have even put a few that work for me in the appendix.

After the first marathon, many runners tend to do another one, but with a certain time in mind. Now you are not running a marathon, you are racing a marathon. Now you are entering a different world! There are many ways to run a marathon. I have run along smiling and having the chats. I have had sunny day runs. I have raced and run hard and felt depths of pain and despair. Take your pick; it's all in there.

Have a Little Faith

There are also many ways to get and stay fit that have nothing to do with running. The important thing is that you do something that you like. It is not important that you are fanatical about your exercise. I tend to be fanatical. And now I enter ultra marathons and other activities that would be classed as a bit over the top. That is me. That's not necessary on your journey to being happier in your own skin. Find the right path and the right activities for you and dedicate yourself to them.

Running is not only a release, it's a connect.

Since I entered my first marathon, the whole process has had a massive impact on me. It motivates me, drives me, overwhelms me, and humbles me. Some days it completes me; other days (and quite often), it totally breaks me.

When I entered my first marathon, I really was naïve. I figured that a marathon might be a way to leapfrog becoming a healthier version of me, cutting out a lot of the daily pain.

A level of ignorance can be a good thing, certainly back at the beginning. But when it comes to fitness and health, action is certainly better than inaction. It is easy to stall and procrastinate when the alternative hurts. After several years of living and eating healthy, action rarely hurts me anymore. It's challenging sometimes and exciting, but the daily pain eventually became pleasure and created a wonderful feeling of well-being. What I liked and didn't like ten years ago has very little to do with the person I am today. Looking at life through a healthy body changes everything.

Good or bad habits deliver results.

Over time, your *why* gets into your bones, the habits you've adopted become a new normal, and you can see the faith in your future materializing. The work you've put in pays off when you watch your life transform before your eyes. It's these habits, these commitments, this new way of living that becomes sustainable over the long haul.

VENICE, ITALY, 27TH OCTOBER 2013
(MY 4TH MARATHON)

It was hot and humid. Five of us had travelled together from Dublin. The night before the marathon, we sat in a local restaurant just by the finish line. The beauty of Venice is inescapable. Romance is in every canal, every building. I was immediately sorry that I was sharing a room with two male friends. Of all the trips, this is the one to take with your partner. I had been so focused on the marathon it hadn't crossed my mind that it was going to be romantic.

There is a one-hour time difference between Dublin and Venice. Coincidentally, the clocks changed back one hour the night before the race in both Ireland and Italy because of Daylight Savings Time. In our tiredness and excitement, we couldn't agree if the clocks went forward or back. For a while, we had no idea what time it was. A bus was scheduled to pick us up the following morning and take us 23 miles out of the city to the start line. With a lot of help, we managed to make the bus on time.

As the sun came up, so did the temperature. We ran a very uneventful plain industrial route towards Venice. At one point the temperature hit 21°C with 100% humidity. When we hit the Ponte della Libertà Bridge, I got a surge of energy. This is almost a two-and-a-half-mile bridge leading from the mainland to the islands of Venice. It signalled the beginning of the end of the race. Six miles to go, possibly the most stunning six miles of any city marathon, anywhere.

I got to within fifty metres of the first island when my body buckled. It just ground to a halt. Muscles seized up, and my body refused to work. I had come off the bridge and run straight into "the wall." I had only heard about "the wall" up to this point. Now I had to see what I was made of. To run through "the wall" is excruciatingly painful.

At this point in the race there were fourteen bridges that still needed to be crossed. Each had been covered with a temporary ramp for the race. At least we didn't have to negotiate steps. The downside was that the temporary structures were very narrow and congested, and we had to break stride to go over them.

Start. Stop. Start. Stop.

It was agonisingly hard work. I had read that the last few miles are so beautiful that they will carry the marathon runners to the finish line. They didn't carry me. I couldn't care less about the scenery at that point. When I realised I was going to miss finishing in under 4 hours, I was devastated. I spotted a small boat in the water, and for a moment I contemplated jumping in and staying there the rest of my life, or rowing away—where to I didn't care. I hadn't enough spare oxygen for that much thought.

With half a mile to go, we entered St. Mark's Square. I tried not to think. It wasn't hard. Everything was about movement.

Don't faint. Don't stop. Just move, move, move. It will end soon.

And it did: 4 hours, 1 minute, and 52 seconds from when I started.

The next two days recovering in the bars, restaurants, and coffee shops of Venice was an absolute treat. I had learnt a bit about myself, and after a few beers, I was even able to pretend to the others that I was over my disappointment about not running a sub 4-hour marathon. Truth was, it just focused me on my next goal.

BENEFITS

Your beliefs become your thoughts,
Your thoughts become your words,
Your words become your actions,
Your actions become your habits,
Your habits become your values,
Your values become your destiny.

Mahatma Gandhi

The Power of Habit

The benefits of feeling good in my own skin aren't always clear. Sometimes I have to look for them. When I do, I see them. One day I looked back at the changes in my life, some subtle and some more obvious, and thanked the old me for having the drive to act and the discipline to stay focused.

The first year of running was more about survival than running, or health, or anything else. It was hard to focus on the overall picture of becoming a strong, healthy, clear-minded sex machine when I was hanging over the neighbour's hedge throwing up.

You get what you expect.

I decided I was running three nights a week regardless of the weather or how I was feeling. And it did feel bad some days, terrible a lot of days, even torturous sometimes. My mind was in constant turmoil. It would tell me it would be okay to miss the run today because it's Monday. There might be a programme on the TV that I shouldn't miss. That niggle in my leg was a defective bone about to snap. And so on and so on. To dismiss myself and go outside and run was a constant struggle. "This is what I do," I kept telling myself. "When I get back, I will review it." But when I got back, I always felt better than I felt before the run, a bit proud of myself and slightly smug that I had beaten the negative fat me once again. I discovered that trying to change my life was going to take a lot of energy.

The benefits of the "power of habit" started to work on me. It took me three months to be able to complete that three-mile loop without walking. It took another nine months before I felt good at it.

The Power of Pushing Boundaries

One of my brothers talked me into entering a triathlon. I am forever grateful, as it was around that event that I got a taste for pushing boundaries. They called it a Sprint Triathlon: a 500 metre swim, 20 km cycle, and a 5 km run. I didn't own a bicycle, and I couldn't swim very well, so for the next six weeks, while continuing to run three times a week, I went to the local pool twice a week and taught myself to swim in a straight line.

As always in life, the dreaded day arrived. We had to swim 50 yards to the starting line and tread water until the hooter sounded. My training in a pool with lines to follow and clear blue water seemed a long way from this lake. A few times I looked up and realised I was going the wrong direction. I got out of the lake shocked and dizzy and fell over while struggling to get my wetsuit off. I felt bruised from being kicked and elbowed, but I was still there. I needed a pee and ran half naked down the road and jumped over a hedge. Later I learned that the seasoned triathletes cover their bodies in baby oil to slip out of the wetsuit.

When I got off the bike, I was still dizzy and a little annoyed that the ambulance shadowed me for the full 20km. Going from the bicycle to running is a very strange experience. I felt like my arms were flailing around independently, like a cartoon character. I ran across the finish line second last. Anyone looking at me might have been puzzled at the big happy head on me. But I had beaten two people—a stranger and the only real person that mattered, the inner me, that constantly harassed me and tried to get me to stop. I was taken aback by the number of people who had waited to cheer the last two runners in. This was the day I learnt that no one will laugh at you for coming in last. In fact, you get more respect for not giving up when you are clearly struggling.

Three months later, my second triathlon was a better story. I managed to climb up from second last to twentieth from last. I still couldn't run and chat at the same time. I told myself that I wasn't very chatty anyway and that "chatting while running" was probably just a myth. I was starting to feel like I might be able to become a fit, slim, healthy version of me. The vision started to become a little clearer. The benefits felt better than I ever expected. I felt good. I felt mentally and physically good.

The Power of a Support System

The next step in pushing my boundaries was connecting with other runners. I helped set up a running group, and we planned to run twice a week at a slow pace. On day one there were eighteen of us. The target was two miles. We walked and ran. After a few weeks we were down to eight runners. The discipline was probably too tough for most. After four weeks we increased our distance to three miles. When we managed to run three miles without stopping, we felt like we could do anything. After eight weeks, those of us still turning up and running decided on a challenge: a half marathon. We got a three-month plan from the Internet, The Half Marathon Roadmap[1] by Matt Frazier, and stuck to it as best we could. Our run of choice

---

1   http://www.nomeatathlete.com/

was the Burren Half Marathon, Co. Clare, known as a "hilly" race. Maybe we should have chosen something that didn't run up the side of a mountain for our first race. As it happened, I couldn't make the race, and the reports were varied. Nine years later they are still talking about the hills!

The second year was easier than the first, but it was still nowhere near easy. The benefits were now clearer, and I felt that when I set my mind on something, I could actually achieve it. My confidence, self-aware-ness, and physical abilities were on the increase. I was waiting for the day that running would be effortless and easy. I'm still waiting.

I was, however, starting to enjoy myself, still slightly in awe of this new, healthy me. I even learnt to run and chat simultaneously. Training with others is so much easier than training alone. When I got to year three, I ran because that's what I expected me to do. If I stopped for a few weeks, my wife would say, "Go for a run, you lazy arse." Even my wife saw me as a runner. That made me feel good. My expectations of myself were now very different than three fat years earlier. I was running regularly without question. I lifted weights and gravitated towards being active. I was always training, sometimes for a half or full marathon, never very seriously, but always moving.

The Power of Proper Nutrition

With an established three times per week training plan, I knew I couldn't out-train a bad diet. I needed to lose weight. I wanted to be fuller for longer and have plenty of energy for my training. I needed slow-release carbohydrates to do that. I adopted the "white is shite" rule, throwing out everything white (rice, pasta, bread) and replacing it with brown. (I still stick by this, nine years on.)

I was eating better every year and cutting back on processed foods and dairy. Whether I took something out or added something into my diet, if it didn't make me feel better, I reversed it. A lot of things I tried came from the books I was reading. I was also learning a lot from the company I was keeping. I was including many things in my smoothies I had never even heard of before I started on my "healthy me" journey—things like spirulina, chia seeds, wheat grass powder, açai powder, maca powder, vegan protein powder, and cacao nibs.

> **You are the average of the five people
> you spend the most time with.**
>
> Jim Rohn

One day I picked up *The China Study*, a book by T. Colin Campbell and his son Thomas Campbell. The book examines the relationship between the consumption of animal products (including dairy) and a list of chronic illnesses such as coronary heart disease, diabetes, breast cancer, prostate cancer, and bowel cancer. The book is partially based on a twenty-year study. The research was so compelling I stopped eating meat altogether, much to my (vegetarian) kids' delight. It was odd that everyone around me suddenly became concerned about me, especially regarding my protein intake. Hardly a week passed without someone asking me, "Do you think it's a good idea to give up meat?" Or they'd ask, "Where are you going to get your protein?"

The first thing I noticed about not eating meat was that I could run any day. Before, if I had a steak on a Wednesday, on Saturday I still couldn't run over ten miles without getting a stitch. I wasn't aware of the three-day process it takes the human body to digest meat. Once I gave up eating meat, it was all too clear. Then I realised that any fruit or vegetables that I consumed after eating meat, fermented and rotted in my system, waiting for their turn to digest after the meat. The thought of any food rotting inside me for days really didn't make me feel good about myself. Through experience, I now know that I feel best on foods that spend the least amount of time in my body—fruits and vegetables being the most obvious.

The next thing I noticed was that I started to lose weight every week. Not much, just about a pound, but it was consistent for the first few months.

Thirdly, and most importantly for me, I felt more alert and had to keep my mouth shut because I wanted to tell everyone. I also knew no one wanted to know. Just because I felt it didn't mean anyone else wanted to hear it. A friend of mine used to say, "What fad are you on this week?"

In time, I learned to brush off such negative comments. I felt trimmer and slimmer. Running was less laboured, always made me feel good, and gave me more energy. At that time, that was all that mattered. I was beginning to live the life I'd longed for, I was feeling better all the time, and I saw I had so much to be grateful for.

TRALEE INTERNATIONAL MARATHON, KERRY, IRELAND, 16TH MARCH 2014 (MY 5TH MARATHON)

This was a new marathon, only in its second year. Five of us headed south from Dublin, full of the usual pre-race mixture of nerves and excitement. The organisers claimed it was one of the most scenic routes in Europe. Once again, I was aiming to run the marathon in under 4 hours, and any bit of scenic help was welcome. Six months earlier I tried to break 4 hours in Venice, only to miss it by 1 minute 52 seconds. I was bitterly disappointed. Over and over I told myself: today was going to be my day. The four-hour mark was not going to get away from me. No, not today!

In Venice, I ran out of everything with a few miles to go and pulled energy out of unknown places just to finish. For those last two miles I felt pain like I hadn't known before. The pain of running on empty is immense. However, it's temporary. Six months of training and planning for Venice and I missed it by 1 minute 52 seconds. It wasn't the only heartbreak I have suffered on my road to beat 4 hours.

Standing in Tralee in the fog and rain felt like a regular Saturday training run—except I was never going to forget this day. With only 345 participants in the race it was going to be a different experience to the usual 10,000 to 20,000. My friend Maeve, from Tralee, had put us up and introduced/assimilated us into her family. It appeared she was related to half the town. My memories of that day are clear, unlike the fog that didn't lift and left me unable to see the view. It was dull, wet, and gloomy.

At Mile 7 I felt fantastic. Somewhere around Mile 12 there was a killer hill. When you get down the far side, you go around a small roundabout and head back up over the same hill again. Really? The thing about the middle of a race is you can throw out as many of those *Really's* as you like. There is no one listening. You're on your own. I really felt it that day. Really.

In many races there is a pacer. Someone who runs the race at a certain pace. If you stick with this pacer, you will finish the race within a certain time. In Venice I spent twenty-four miles of the race running ahead of the 4-hour pacer. He had a large red balloon strapped to his back with 04:00 on it. The first twenty-three miles of the race, I thought he was going too slow for me, so I ran ahead. With about two miles to go, while I ran over a narrow bridge, the pacer passed me. Not only that—as he passed, his balloon struck me on the side of the head. It was like being hit with a wet plank. My knees almost buckled with the blow.

I had been so sure I would make it in under 4 hours. Where had I gone wrong? Watching the pacer leave me behind with every stride made me feel like I was stuck in a slow-motion dream. I felt shattered.

Here I was, running ahead of the 4-hour pacer again in Tralee. I hoped it wasn't a mistake.

Listen to everyone, follow no one.

Dean Karnazes

I spent over five miles running along the Kerry coast. Alone. At one stage, a man appeared and passed me, soon disappearing into the fog.

The previous day I'd telephoned a friend and sports psychologist, Neil O'Brien, and told him I was afraid I would fall apart with only a few miles to go. I asked if he could help. Without hesitation he said, "Yes, that's no problem," and gave me several things to focus on when the going got tough. We went through a few mental techniques to prevent me from imploding.

The first 3 hours passed reasonably well. I felt comfortable and hopeful. At one stage you run onto a pier, go around a traffic cone, and run back on the other side. There was a small black marquee tent that looked like it might blow away any second. It was housing a man, a table and chair, a microphone, and a list. I ran past him, and we nodded a greeting at each other. It was good to see another human. It was good to know I hadn't run off course. We were the only two people on the pier, and as I passed him on my way back, he had obviously looked at my number (35) and found me on his list. Out of the speakers blasted "Jonathan Cairns, number 35." It made me smile. It's always reassuring to get confirmation about who you are and what your number is.

When Mile 21 appeared, I was getting nervous, I was slowing down; my energy was draining fast. I looked over my shoulder and saw the 4-hour pacer coming up behind me. My heart sank. I could feel the power draining out of my legs. *No, not again. No. No. No.* I felt my right knee buckle, and I stuttered to a limp. The pacer and a few dozen runners passed me.

I went deep into my gut and told myself that limp or not, I was going to finish this race in under 4 hours. I asked myself, *How badly do you want this? Do it now. Embrace the pain.* I went through a pre-rehearsed mantra in my head as Neil had instructed me. I tried to rid my mind of all thoughts and concentrated on one sentence only. I blocked out every other thought and feeling, negative or otherwise.

I am strong. I am trained. I am ready for this.
I am strong. I am trained. I am ready for this.

I repeated these words to myself over and over.

I changed my pace to the beat of this sentence. I fought to block the pain. I started to move again. Two miles later, I caught sight of the 4-hour group. I was closing the gap. My knee hadn't snapped. I had almost caught the pacer group by Mile 25. Everything in me wanted to stop and take a rest. I refused to face it. I wouldn't look. I can only describe it as blind pain. All thoughts and feelings were moved to my head only. I was prepared to collapse before I let this get away from me. My legs felt like they belonged to someone else.

As I passed the group, just coming up to 25 and a half miles, the pacer turned and said to me, "Have you ever beaten the 4 hours before?" I shook my head, afraid to speak in case my insides spilled out. He said, "You're going to beat it today."

The words filled me. I came around the last bend as if in someone else's body. I ran as fast as the legs I was attached to could take me. I was trying not to think and terrified that I might fall over. Myself and my body crossed the line with 53 seconds to spare.

Most people have no idea how good their body is designed to feel.

Kevin Trudeau

The following day I awoke feeling elated and tired. On the inside I felt like dancing. Knowing how bad a dancer I am, I kept it inside. It was a clear day, so we drove the marathon route and got to appreciate the magnificent coastline we had missed the previous day. Afterward, we headed home to Dublin. I arrived back to my family the same on the outside. But inside I was a different man. I was now a sub 4-hour marathon runner. I wondered if they could tell by looking at me.

GRATITUDE

It's Never too Late to Feel Better

I'm not sure if we are living longer these days, but we are dying longer.

Appreciation for the moment is now something I practice regularly. I try and appreciate having working arms and legs and a healthy heart and lungs that beat blood and oxygen to all my muscles. I am grateful that I can run up a mountain and feel the pain in my legs and the wind and cold rain on my face. I am grateful for waking feeling healthy, and I now appreciate my life. I never had this before I started running. I'm not saying you will, just that I do.

The benefits of practising gratitude are nearly endless. The process fills me with a sense of warmth and calm. I take the time to notice the small things I'm grateful for every day. The things that make me happy to be here. Some are very big and easy to notice, like when my kids smile at me. But I try and focus on the small things too: a conversation, a great cup of coffee, the ability to skip up the stairs, a fabulous taste, to name but a few. Like a lot of things, noticing is just a habit. I find when I take the time to be grateful, I come at everything from a better place.

It took me several marathons to learn to take the time to appreciate just where I was and how far I had come. Just standing on the starting line before an event I always try to be grateful for just being there. Regardless of what happens next, I tell myself, "I'm here, how bad?" I try to enjoy the whole race, not just the finish. And I appreciate that I am sharing this space with hundreds, sometimes thousands, of like-minded people. Total strangers even shout encouragement and offer water and food en route. It's almost overwhelming some days.

It doesn't always work, and I get caught up in the race sometimes, but I try to be present.

Trade expectation for gratitude.

One morning I was in the hospital, and a patient asked me to tell her about my weekend. I was reluctant to. She is a runner, now paralysed from a car accident and confined to a chair. She looked me boldly in the eye and said, "Please."

I sat down, and she held my finger between her working thumb and forefinger. If she thought I was holding back, she squeezed with force. We both smiled at this setup, and I told her all about my ten-mile run the previous morning with my running partner Emma. I told of the autumn leaves in the park, the cold gusting wind, the salty sweat in my eyes, even the conversation we had while running. We had run through Phoenix Park, through the forest down by the lakes, and up to the US Ambassador's residence. A few times we passed a herd of deer.

She closed her eyes as I spoke, and tears ran down her face. When I finished, I wiped my own tears and got up and left the room without another word, feeling a bit ashamed that I had ever complained about anything in my life.

There are times when we run, and breezes from a
whole different world begin to whisper.

DUBLIN MARATHON, IRELAND, 27TH OCTOBER 2014 (MY 6TH MARATHON)

Deciding to run a marathon is a big day. Almost as big as the race day. I have seen people line up on the starting line dressed in the most ridiculous of outfits: a mankini, a fireman's outfit, a Barney suit, even a cardboard box. The reality is a marathon is hundreds of miles, the 26.2 are just the last bit. And, really, who is qualified to call someone else crazy? Certainly no one in the race.

I have run marathons and wondered about death, even wished for death. I have run marathons and thanked the universe for giving me the opportunity to feel so alive. I have looked back and said I should have been more prepared. I should have trained differently. I should have respected the distance more. "I will be grand" just doesn't cut it for a race of 26.2 miles. (I have tried. It doesn't work.) But I have never looked back and said, "I wish I hadn't lifted my fat arse off the chair and trained for that marathon." Not yet anyway.

Dublin 2014 was probably my greatest disaster so far. I can go there in an instant. I had run a sub 4-hour marathon six months earlier in Tralee. I was sure that running marathons in over 4 hours was behind me. From now on, I was only going to get faster and faster. Surely.

Discipline is how we manifest ourselves to the world.

I had only one goal—mistake number one. My goal was to finish in or around 3 hours and 50 minutes. I started with the 3-hour 50 pacer, a small slight man with a large white balloon tied to his waist. The first ten miles, I was feeling good. Miles 11 and 12 were just a bad patch, I thought as I started to feel sluggish and tired. On Mile 13,

I knew I was screwed. The pacer started to leave me, and I couldn't get my breathing right.

Fiona and my son Jem were at Mile 15, and I felt like death as I passed by. Jem ran a few hundred metres with me. I had run the first half of the race too fast and was paying for it. From that point on, every step was painful. Soon after, every breath.

At Mile 22 I met my friend Laura. We had run the Dublin marathon together the previous year, so I couldn't look her in the eye.

On Mile 23 I felt like I was running in slow motion. I saw some friends and family, and I felt embarrassed at having got it so wrong.

I hit Mile 25 feeling like a dead man running. *Why am I running this race? Why am I alive? What is the meaning of this life? What's the point in this much suffering?* I stopped and walked bits. I was dizzy and found it hard to focus. I didn't know or care where I was.

I crossed the finish line with a time of 4 hours 24 minutes—a full 25 minutes slower than my previous marathon.

When you're so focused on the event, it can be hard to realise that no one cares about your time except you. People come to support you, not judge you. A few of us met after the race in a local pub for some food and refreshments. I remember sitting on the stairs for a few minutes, head in my hands, weak and trying to recover. What a screw-up. I found out that day that you are only as good as your training. I made a promise to myself that I would never again start a marathon undertrained. (If only I had stuck to it.) I had trained half-heartedly and skipped many long runs. I thought the fitness in my body from six months earlier would still carry me.

Confidence is a big thing when it comes to running. It takes confidence to trust yourself. To trust yourself takes training and practice. The variables that exist over those twenty-six miles are many. Am I starting out too fast? Did I drink enough water? Did I drink too much? Is the course hillier than I anticipated? If the sun comes out and I start to heat up, have I the ability to recalculate my race goal? Can I drop my ego and go to plan B or C?

The Dublin Marathon in 2014 was a big lesson for me. On that day I learnt a few things that will hopefully stay with me forever.

The first: wishful thinking doesn't count for anything. You do the work, or you pay the price. And it's a very high price.

The second: success is never given; it's earned.

The third: the runs that almost break you can be the runs that make you.

I now had two choices: stop running marathons or run them properly. I didn't fancy stopping on a personal failure, so I looked up another marathon to enter.

THE BEGINNING

Everything starts somewhere, although many physicists disagree.

Hogfather, Terry Pratchett

The Book of Genesis

They say running a marathon changes you. It doesn't. Being separated from your children changes you. Going from being with your kids every day to every second weekend changes you. A void splits your gut open so wide you struggle to hold yourself together.

To combat this pain, I started to do something that hurt: I ran, if you could call it that. Under a cloud of darkness, I'd place one foot in front of the other and move. It was somewhere between a shuffle and falling. I coughed, shuffled, and spluttered my way around the neighbourhood. Sometimes strangers would ask if I was okay. I was told I looked like a wounded bear. Wounded I certainly was.

On Sunday evenings I used to drop my three kids back to their mother. It used to break my heart. I was afraid for them. Afraid that I was leaving them with a depressed woman who hadn't the equipment to put their needs before hers. The guilt was crippling. I knew there wasn't enough vodka on the planet for me to kill the pain, so after I dropped them, I used to run, sometimes aimlessly, until my legs and lungs would take me no farther. It never took long, but by the time I got home, the edge had been knocked off. I couldn't sleep much, and I felt like a fog had been pulled over me for a long time. After a few months of jogging on Sunday nights, I started to chance running during the week.

From my house, I mapped a three-mile loop, the first mile uphill. My target was to run it in one go without stopping—and live. I walked and ran, walked and ran for three miles. In the first month, I was convinced I would never become a runner. It didn't bother me much—I didn't want to be. It was pure therapy, with side effects.

There was something else too. I had spotted a photograph of myself, and I was horrified. I had been looking through photographs of my kids to put on the wall when I came across one particular photo of me. I asked my partner, "Is that what I look like?" When she answered yes, my attitude towards myself changed. I came into the real world. I stopped thinking, *That's a terrible angle of a picture*. I saw myself as I really was. A fucking elephant.

I wondered why no one had told me I looked a few stone overweight and one bite away from a heart attack. I have since been told that it had been pointed out to me and I just wasn't ready to hear it. Maybe the people around me were too polite. Maybe they thought I was too sensitive to hear something so direct. Are we ever ready to hear that the way we're living is hurting us and making us unhealthy? I recall only one woman, my sister-in-law, who I hadn't seen in five or six years saying to me, "Oh my God, J, you got so fat." I didn't like it then, but I appreciate it now. Perhaps no one realises that you haven't noticed. I said to my brother recently, "Why didn't you tell me I was getting fat?" He replied, "I wasn't aware you had no mirrors at home."

The secret of getting ahead is getting started.
The secret of getting started is breaking your complex,
overwhelming tasks into small manageable tasks,
and then starting on the first one.

Mark Twain, author

Find a Place to Start

Running from a standing start, a place of no exercise, is very hard. Yet there is no other way to start than to put on your gear and run, walk, jog, shuffle—anything, just move. You think you look weak, feeble, incompetent, pathetic. In fact, if anyone even notices you as you head out your door and down your street (it's likely they don't notice you, by the way), you look like a runner. And when they see you, they're probably not thinking how weak and pathetic you look. They're more likely to feel jealous that you are out running and they are not.

We do not see things as they are, we see things as we are.

Anaïs Nin

I found breathing particularly difficult in those early days. And a feeling of total exhaustion, mental and physical, was a common occurrence for me, even after running only small distances. Being an ex-smoker didn't help either, I'm sure. For the first month, I sweated and huffed and puffed. Getting a deep breath was a problem. My chest tightened like it was caving in, and I always struggled to have enough energy. Walking 2 minutes and running 30 seconds was the only way I could manage. Slowly, I started to reduce the walking time. After many runs, I changed to jogging 5 minutes walking 15 seconds. There was no sign of it getting any easier; it still took everything, and it hurt like hell.

A few months into my attempted jogging, I entered a local 5k race. I felt I had no choice. The starting line was 20 metres from my house. Being the fool I am, I was so excited I started up the front and ran as fast as I could for the first kilometre. I got about 200 metres before I knew I had made a mistake. My legs grew heavy, and my energy started to evaporate. The next few kilometres I thought about how ridiculous running was and how utterly pointless and dangerous it was. I tried to latch on to some slow runners, but I couldn't keep up. Everyone seemed to be passing me. At the 4-kilometre mark I was going to pass my house, and to save the embarrassment of dropping dead, I planned to run in my front door. When I got there, there were a few people I knew standing outside my house, and they started clapping and shouting encouragement once they saw me. I kept going and headed into the last kilometre utterly exhausted and breathless. With half a kilometre to go, I still didn't know if I could make the finish. I repeated to myself, *Run, Jesus, run, you fat pr*ck.* I ran as hard as I could through a lot of pain, then it was over. I crossed the line and was handed a bottle of water and a banana.

I'd told myself, *If I get over the pain of running and out of this race unmaimed, I'm never going to run again.* It didn't work out that way. Something odd happened. After the race, I felt a little bit good about myself. Good that I hadn't given up, and focused on the fact that I finished. I liked that feeling, and I liked being around so many positive people. Fiona had commented that almost everybody racing looked well and slim.

They sure did. I wanted to be one of them.

Find a Way to Keep Going

The following year when the race came around again, I took a moment to look at myself. I had now spent over twelve months huffing and puffing. I was still overweight, but I was looking and feeling better. I was working out and, most importantly, I was still running. Friends stopped asking me out on a Friday night because they knew I wouldn't go because of my Saturday morning run. It dawned on me that time was going to pass regardless of what I did. I thought, *Why not make the most of every week and get fitter and stronger and be a better version of me come this same race next year?* I realised that how I would be this time next year depended on what I did between now and then.

I wanted to look back and say, "What a great year! I made the most of it, and look what I achieved." My eating habits started to change. Just by acting healthier I wanted to eat healthier. Every time it came to shoving something into my mouth, more often than not, I wanted it to be on the healthy side.

After the first 5k race, I continued running the three-mile loop from my house three times a week. Every single run was still a hardship. I sweated buckets and really suffered with my breathing. After a few months, I managed to run three miles without stopping.

Discovering How Much I Didn't Know

Knowing little or nothing about running, and less about myself, I went online and entered the Rome Marathon. It was far enough away that I wouldn't know anyone, yet I could get there in only a few hours. Still running under a cloud of darkness, I trained three times a week. Just by entering and booking flights, I thought I would be a better runner. It didn't quite work like that.

Fiona decided a weekend in Rome would be fun, so she signed up for the marathon too. Not the training. She wasn't big on training back then. The long training runs were painful, and I often skipped them. I also thought if I ran a marathon, the small runs like the three-mile loop from my house would become easy. I thought that a few intense months of training would elevate me to another level, give me a shortcut to mental and physical well-being. Not for the first time in my life, I was wrong.

Going to the gym can be tough, but without good form and guidance you can waste a lot of time working out. I found with running, there is no hiding. There is something very honest about running. There is very little gear and stuff, so I couldn't even waste time trying to look good. There is no looking good. You put the work in, and you trust you get the reward out. The first year was most definitely the hardest. In year two, the rewards came a bit quicker. As I started to get fitter, minor injuries became less frequent. Friends noticed I looked healthier, my energy levels jumped, and I found self-confidence; I could actually do this. I kept my discipline, and I kept giving myself targets, 5k and 10k races to enter. I liked the new, slimmer, more energetic me.

Expect as much success as you have discipline.

Caleb Cairns

Start at the Beginning

This parable is told of a farmer who owned an old mule. The mule fell into the farmer's well. The farmer heard the mule braying, or whatever mules do when they fall into wells. After carefully assessing the situation, the farmer sympathised with the old mule but decided that neither the mule nor the well was worth the trouble of saving. Instead, he called his neighbours together, told them what had happened, and enlisted them to help haul dirt to bury the old mule in the well and put him out of his misery. As shovel after shovel of dirt fell on his back, he brayed hysterically. But as the farmer and his neighbours continued shovelling and the dirt hit his back, it dawned on the old mule that every time a load of dirt landed on his back, he would shake it off and step up.

This he did, blow after blow. Shake it off and step up. Shake it off and step up. Shake it off and step up. It wasn't long before the old mule, distressed and exhausted, stepped triumphantly over the wall of the well. What seemed like it would bury him, actually helped him. All because of the manner in which he handled his adversity.

Take from that what you like. To me it says, face your problems.

Refuse to give in to panic, bitterness, or self-pity and good sh*t will happen.

For me the first step was in my head. I decided that I was going to get fit. I needed to channel the pain of loss, and I needed to take some form of control over my life. I chose running. No membership. No expensive equipment. No embarrassment in front of others. Of course, there is no embarrassment in making yourself a better person, regardless of what shape you are in.

Once I decided to put on running shoes and go out the front door, I was in a better place. I wasn't quite a better man, but I was definitely in a better place. It then became about ritual and routine. Discipline does not come easy, and routine plays a big part. Focusing on the week I was in was very important. It started with one session at a time. Every walk, run, jog was a big deal. I never looked past the next session.

Every day I said to myself, "You want to change? What's stopping you? You will never change your life until you change something you do daily. Geese don't need to fly South."

Nothing changes until you do.

Mike Robbins

Finding Your Starting Point

Let me share with you a four-step plan for getting started. If I boil down my experience into steps, it would look something like this:

Step 1: Wherever you are in your life, get off the pity pot (as the Americans say).

If you are feeling a little bit sorry for yourself, put it aside. You can feel sorry for yourself another day. Right now, you're going to take the first step away from pity.

Accept your sh*t. If you can't accept it, put it aside. You can deal with it later. Right now, you're going to take the first step away from sh*t.

Take responsibility for your life. If you can't take responsibility, put the blame aside. You can deal with the blame later. Right now, you're going to take the first step away from blame.

From this moment on, that means today, become accountable for everything that happens to you. Good and bad. Oh, and if you can't be accountable, just take steps two, three, and four below and leave the accountability to the plan.

Step 2: Make a plan.

There are three running plans at the end of the book you can choose from.

Have you ever said, "I couldn't run a _____?" (insert race distance you think you couldn't run). Have you ever wondered why you have placed that limiting belief on yourself? Now's the time to smash that wide open. The running plans included will help you to:

- Run your first 5k
- Run your first half marathon
- Run your first marathon

If you don't like any of these, make up your own. Swap running for rowing. Don't fancy just running every week? Then mix it up and do one run, one cycle, one swim a week instead. With a 5k distance, the object is rarely to win, it's to look and feel good. If you can have fun on the way, how bad?

Step 3: Act.

I've suggested running plans because I know they work. I've followed them, and I've run those distances as a result of following simple plans like these. People I know have followed them, and they too have run longer and stronger as a result. They are flexible and easy to follow.

Can't do a long run on a Sunday but can on a Monday? Change it. Prefer to run before work in the morning? Run early. If the plan schedules three runs a week then do three runs a week. The most important thing is consistency.

In our house, we stick a calendar on the back of the kitchen door that shows the entire year.[2] I circle the big events I am going to train for during the year and plan my training to get me to the start line prepared. If I have a sixteen-week training plan for a marathon, I count back sixteen weeks and highlight the start date. I then write each of the distances of the scheduled run on the calendar for the entire sixteen-week training plan. This helps me to keep on track for my goal. Each time I complete a run, I tick it off. If I miss a run, I cross it out and see if I can fit it in on another day that week. It is satisfying to see progress as a sequence of ticks on the calendar.

---

2   You can find one like it at https://www.octagon-design.com/shop/vertical-calendar-2016.

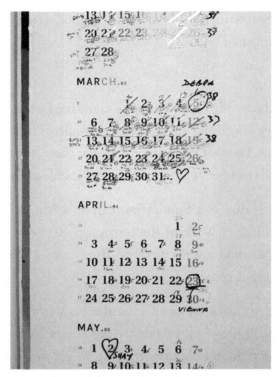

Training calendar for the 2017 Vienna Marathon

Step 4: Stick to your plan.

This is the most important step. You can want to get fitter/healthier/
sexier/happier, but it can't happen unless you act (step 3 and step 4),
and keep acting by sticking to your plan. An average plan that you
act on is much better than an amazing plan that you do not act on.

If your problem is weight, take a moment and think how many years
of inattentive eating and lack of exercise got you to the weight you
are today. Did you go off-track after a bad breakup last year? Have
you put on more and more weight each year since you had kids?
Have years of working as a sales rep, sitting in your car, and eating
fast food made you the shape you are today? Don't get hung up on
the scales. Keep one eye on the overall picture. The scales will look
after themselves.

If it has taken you months or years to get here, do you really think you can solve it all by writing out a plan and signing up to a new gym membership before throwing in the towel and claiming failure? No one said it was going to be a piece of cake. It will be hard. I know. I've been there. It's why the "why" is so important. If you can't remember why you're doing it, flip back to the 35 reasons why you should read this book and remind yourself why you're doing this now.

Note to self: Remember, sh*t happens. Sometimes life will get in the way. That's okay. Just pick up where you left off. And try not to take yourself too seriously. This can be fun.

The race is long and, in the end, it's only with yourself.

Mary Schmich

Get Your Head in the Game

Get into the right headspace. Take a look at yourself. Take your clothes off. Weigh yourself and take three measurements. You might need help with this.

1. Step on a scales.

Measure:

2. Around your back and under your arms, across your chest and nipples.

3. Around your waist to your belly button.

4. Around your hips and buttocks.

Record these measurements. They will become a source of inspiration. Repeat once a month.

Decide what weight you would like to be. Write it down and stick it on your fridge. I put a finish date on mine. I didn't want this to be ongoing. Don't open that fridge again without looking at your post.

Understand your purpose. Mine was: "I will get fit and stop eating crap."

Make your decision public. What you decide now will have repercussions for your whole family and maybe for the rest of your life. Let your partner know what's going on and try to rope in everyone around you. I started my journey alone, but in time I had training partners that helped keep me on track. Having someone to train with makes it easier. It's harder to make an excuse to get out of your long run on Saturday when someone else is relying on you to be there.

Make a plan. If it can't be broken down, it will be too difficult. In my case, it was important that I aimed for something big enough to excite me but not too big to be unattainable.

Here's a copy of my first plan:

> **9th January 2008**
> **Run/walk 3 miles, 3 nights per/week (no excuses)**
> **Give up fizzy drinks**
> **Weigh 91 kg**

That was it. My first plan. I wrote it down. I signed it. I stuck to it. And when May came around, I was ready for a new plan.

> **2nd May 2008**
> **Run 3 miles, 3 times per week (no excuses)**
> **Spend 15 minutes after each run doing press ups & stretches**
> **Give up WHITE—bread, pasta, rice**
> **Juice vegetables daily**
> **Weigh 81 kg**

Just like the first plan, I wrote it down and signed it. If I wasn't going to be accountable to a training partner, I was going to be accountable to myself.

The first few months were incredibly tough, and I only ran at night. I was too self-conscious to be seen around the neighbourhood. The second few months got harder. The improvements happened in jumps, and there were long periods when I felt I was going nowhere. It took me another year to realise that no one notices you when you are running. More importantly, no one cares.

That might not be your hang-up. You may have your own, different from mine. But it's likely you have something holding you back, niggling at the edges of your mind. Don't let it get you down. Here are a few tips you may find come in handy as you begin.

Beginner Tips I've Learnt along the Way

- **If in doubt about anything, just put on your running shoes and get out the front door.** Action always wins.
- **Find an exercise you love.** It makes being active feel so good.
- **Don't be afraid of fear.** Fear can be crippling, even when unfounded.
- **Don't overcomplicate things.** Just start. Now.
- **Confidence is a mood.** Be confident.
- **Don't food shop when you're hungry.** Prime time for bad choices.
- **Drink your coffee black with no sugar.** The fewer dairy products in your system the better, and sugar makes you feel hungry sooner.
- **Start with one small change.** Then own it and be proud of it before adding another.

- **Eat healthy protein (beans, lentils, nuts, fish, eggs).** These make you feel full.

- **Find a healthy meal you like.** It's too hard to eat healthy if you think you don't like the food.

- **Chew more.** It's good for digestion.

- **Avoid sugar.** It causes havoc on your system.

- **Eat complex carbs (brown rice, sweet potatoes, oats).** There's less chance of gaining weight, and these give you sustained energy for longer.

- **Don't skip meals.** This makes you hungry and leads to poor food choices.

- **Replace bad snacks with good snacks.** When bad habits become good habits, everything gets easier.

- **Eat more vegetables and fruit.** Because you're worth it.

- **Lift weights.** It builds stronger muscles and joints and increases your metabolism.

- **Move every day.** When exercise becomes part of your daily life, it ceases to be a chore.

- **Drink water.** Or shrivel up and die.

- **Get rid of junk foods in your house.** If they're not in your cupboard when you want a snack, they are easier to avoid.

- **Eat good fats (coconut oil, almonds, avocados).** These provide energy, protect your organs, and help absorb vitamins A, D, E, and K.

- **Eat fibre.** Fibre slows the rate that sugar is absorbed into the bloodstream. Luckily when you eat fruit, vegetables, and carbohydrates, you're also getting plenty of fibre.

- **Drink less alcohol.** Where do I start? Always a good idea.

- **Give up one thing at a time.** Start today.

- **The secret to your success is found in your daily routine.** Make a plan.

Another source of trouble for beginners are misconceptions and cultural myths miring them in fear and holding them back from jumping into these new habits. Consider the following mythbusters.

Mythbusters

1. **Certain foods burn fat.**

   Sorry! There is no such thing as fat-burning foods. You can throw out your "top 5 fat burning foods" list! You can, however, choose foods that will fill you up and provide you with energy to sustain you. You'll burn plenty of fat through healthy eating and movement.

2. **You can do exercises for a flat stomach.**

   Nope. There are no exercises for a flat stomach. That's right, none. For starters, you cannot dictate where your body loses fat. It will go from wherever it chooses to—and at a speed that is different for everyone. However, you can tone your stomach muscles so that when you do lose belly fat, there's a nice six pack underneath.

3. **Eating fast food or cakes and fizzy drinks is a treat.**

   When you eat crap—you feel like crap. The immediate pleasure you get from eating fats and sugars is quickly lost. These empty calories don't fill you up; as a result, you tend to overeat.

4. **You have to eat less to lose weight.**

   Although this may be the case for you, it's also possible you're eating too little and you should try eating more. When it comes to fat loss, you need to burn off more calories than you consume. However, if you consume too few calories, your body goes into starvation mode. Your body stores the calories you eat as fat and, instead, breaks down lean muscle.

5. **You should see your weight come down every week on the scales.**

Wrong! Don't pay too much attention to the scales. This is not an indicator of your health, mood, strength, or progress. Your weight will not trend steadily downwards day by day. Many factors influence your weight. For women, this is true particularly during their menstrual cycle. As long as the *trend* is downwards towards your goal, you're doing fine.

6. **I just don't have the discipline.**

I have discovered that focus and discipline can be built. You can create habits that, like most things, become easier with practice. However, don't expect it to happen overnight. The latest studies have shown that it takes, on average, sixty-six days to create a habit. For most people, that's a little over two months of doing the new practice—every day. Maybe it's not that you don't have the discipline but that you're afraid to fail. Fear of failure is one of the biggest inhibitors of action. What are you afraid of?

DÜSSELDORF MARATHON, GERMANY, 24TH APRIL 2016 (MY 9ᵀᴴ MARATHON)

We left the house that morning with a spring in our step. On the tram heading into Düsseldorf, no one spoke. There was nothing to say.

We thought we were ready. There is a feeling before a race that's a mixture of nerves, fear, and vulnerability. That day, there was also a bit of something else. I think it was confidence.

Christmas three months earlier was always going to be a running Christmas more than a night out, social-type Christmas. I had a training partner and good friend Emma (my running wife) helping me through. We were the same standard and were training for the same marathon, so with a little luck and a lot of discipline we were hoping for a good race time. Training with others is not only more enjoyable, it simply makes you run faster. The previous year in the Düsseldorf marathon, I missed a sub 4-hour finish by 7 seconds. I had a bit of an edge on me this time around.

Training started the first week of January, and the first long run in week one was twelve miles. This meant getting up to twelve miles in the "out of training" time, to be ready for week one. I had scheduled a sixteen-week training program, and it all went to plan. I ate well, slept well, trained hard, and avoided injury. For the first time, I ran four times per week and didn't skip runs.

The day came, and I found myself standing by the Rhine at the starting line. I felt nervous as usual, but ready. Music was playing, and Emma and I started to dance. We must have looked ridiculous. There was no hiding it—we felt good.

Our plan was to run the first twenty-one miles at 8 minutes 45 seconds per mile. If we had anything left in the tank we would reassess and either hold the pace or maybe even speed up. Our first aim was to run a sub 4-hour race. We had trained together for three solid months. I suspected Emma might leave me behind somewhere around Mile 20. She had been looking very sharp the last few weeks.

We were off. No more training, waiting, speculating. In 4 hours—hopefully a little less—we would know exactly where we were at. Düsseldorf is flat, and this day it was cold and dry. Perfect conditions.

At Mile 10 we felt good. Too early to predict a finishing time, but things were looking good.

At Mile 15 we had a brief snow shower. It was lovely. Anything that takes your mind off your body is good.

Mile 20 we saw we had held a steady 8:45 pace and decided to keep it up. I now knew this was going to be a good day.

At Mile 25 just before Emma took off, Fiona stepped out, handed me some dates, and said, "You've got this. You've got this."

In Düsseldorf, the last few hundred yards are gloriously downhill. And with the finish line in sight, I ran to the end, ecstatic. I crossed the finish line, arms held high. My finish time was 3.51.01, 9 minutes 6 seconds faster than my previous attempt. I was filled with such joy I thought I was going to explode. Four months, hundreds of miles, and a target I broke by 9 minutes!

The discipline had paid off.

FUEL

Don't Put Diesel in an Unleaded Tank

I recently listened to a diabetic, unable to walk or use his fingers, tell me that he had no idea how he became diabetic. "It's not in the family," he said. This sixty-four-year-old man didn't understand that his eating habits were connected to his own health.

This level of detachment and ignorance, deliberate or otherwise, is quite common. We have a disconnect between what we eat and the realities of our health. A lot of us still don't think that what we eat and drink leads to health or sickness. Heart disease, we think, is just genetic: "My parents had it." Same with diabetes: "My parents had it." Same with certain types of cancer. It's convenient to think that we have no part in pressing the "on" switch.

It's easy to see how we ended up here. Growing up, we were fed misinformation from our parents, the government, and the food industry. On the TV, young, healthy, good-looking teenagers with polo neck jumpers and white teeth joked around on a pier, laughing and smoking Major cigarettes. As a child, I thought it was cool to smoke cigarettes, healthy to drink milk, and good to eat a Mars Bar a day. "Helps you work rest, and play," the ad said. To think we promoted a healthy lifestyle with tobacco, dairy, and sugar.

A lot of people still don't know which foods are healthy and which foods are not. I don't claim to have the answers either, but I read a lot and make choices that resonate with me. I am happy in the knowledge that I have stopped listening to the people who have an interest in what I buy and started listening to my own body. If you read a study in relation to food, it is important that you get into the habit of looking up who funded it.

There was a time when I would be driving through the countryside and see a cow in a field, and my first thought would be the type of sizzling steak that could be cut from its backside. The hardest part of changing my diet wasn't the not-eating-meat bit. It was, and still is, the changing of my thought process. Changing the way I was brought up to think takes a conscious effort. Seeking out other opinions and test results means continuously questioning what I thought was fact.

Once I started probing, I saw that most information comes from the food industry itself, which makes it untrustworthy, as they are motivated by profit, not health.

How do we know which foods promote health and which foods promote disease?

Is milk just liquid meat, all fat and cholesterol?

Is white meat better than red meat?

Does meat encourage colon, breast, and prostate cancer (to name a few)?

Does sugar feed cancer?

There are also so many conflicting threads of information when it comes to eating "healthy food" that it's extremely difficult to determine what's accurate. When I decided to take control of my health, I read a lot of books about the relationship between what a person eats and the state of their health. I also watched a lot of documentaries. I have listed many of them in the appendices. Three themes carried through the majority of what I came across:

1. Eat more vegetables and fruit.

2. Eat fewer animal products.

3. Avoid processed foods (anything with a label) and sugar-laden

foods.

In a world of false claims, I read everything I can get my hands on, follow none of it, and make my own plans. I pick and choose based purely on what works for me.

The goal, for me, is to be healthy and to feel good most of the time. Once I remember this, there is no conflict or option. I started gradually decreasing the amount of meat in my diet, and after reading *The China Study*, I gave up meat altogether. It's hard to un-know something, and what I read rang so true for me that I didn't choose it—it chose me. Soon after, sugar followed. At the time, I was doing a month of eating a raw food diet, and we made healthy treats that used dates to sweeten them. I found them to be even more delicious than regular cakes and confections.

Keep an Open Mind

Over the years that followed, I gravitated towards being vegan. I eat organic eggs from a local farmer. Occasionally, I eat fish. So, although I avoid all meat and dairy, it doesn't come with a label like *vegan*. I have enough labels. It's no fun being a coeliac sugar-free vegan when you're invited for dinner. Everyone is stumped as to what to make you.

I recently celebrated New Year's Eve with family, and everyone was tasked with bringing a dish. They all agreed to a vegan, gluten-free, sugar-free meal. Fiona and I were bringing dessert. I was inundated with messages asking if this or that was okay and if they could use such-and-such in the dish. But after all the questions were answered, what resulted was a gorgeous Coconut and Sweet Potato soup to start, followed by a Bean Chilli with Baked Potatoes and Salad for the main. For dessert we brought a Chocolate, Orange Tart and an Apple, Pear, and Blackberry Crumble. Sometimes people say that was a nice meat-free meal, as though it was nice *even though* there was no meat in it. But the lack of anything wasn't mentioned on this particular evening, just the yums and umms of a delicious meal. All these recipes and more are included in the My Food Appendix.

There is a phrase I love: *Nobody can do your press-ups for you.* Eating well is the same. Only you can decide what to put into your mouth.

Keeping a food diary is one way to track what you are eating before deciding what changes to make. I worked with a woman a few years ago, and she asked for help losing weight. I told her to keep a food diary for a week and I would sit down with her a week later and look at her meals and snacks and make some suggestions for improvement.

A week later she presented me with a tidy notebook of neatly written, perfectly formed meals and healthy snacks. It was like something you would read in a diary entry for a monk fasting during lent: Brown bread and a boiled egg for breakfast, a soup and salad at lunchtime, some chicken with rice and vegetables for dinner. Carrot sticks with hummus served as her snack. No dessert, no fizzy drinks, no chocolate or sweets. This woman was carrying extra weight, and the diet didn't look like it could support it.

"Is this how you always eat, or was this an unusual week?" I asked.

"No. This is my usual diet," she replied.

I pushed a little more, "Nothing else? No treats, no biscuits with your cup of tea?"

"Oh," she said.

It turned out she'd had back surgery a year prior. Before the surgery the pain would wake her in the middle of the night. She would get up, move a little to ease the pain, and eat a packet of biscuits before returning to bed. Over time this became a habit. Now, post-surgery, and without being woken by pain, her habit was to wake at night and get up. Before it was to ease the pain—now it was to eat the biscuits.

"I think we've found the source of your problem," I said.

Whoever snuck the "s" in "Fast Food" was a clever little b*stard.

Take Responsibility for Your Diet

In the early days, when everyone around me started to notice changes, my mother, mother-in-law, and even some friends got annoyed every time I gave something up. I used to find that I was always having to explain my food choices. Years on, it's not so bad. Every day in the media there are stories acknowledging the links between food and exercise, sickness and death. Choosing the healthy option isn't such a lonely place anymore. It doesn't raise as many eyebrows now that taking responsibility for your own health is more mainstream. Although what I eat is no longer a topic of conversation, people make jokes about themselves when they are eating foods in front of me that they know I wouldn't eat. I find it very funny that they know they are making an unhealthy choice and rather than not eat it, they brush it off as a joke.

The thing about eating is, your body has to digest what you put into it. There is no hiding from it, and there is no one coming to save you. You are the only one responsible for what you eat and, unless you are a child, it doesn't happen to you—you choose it. In the beginning that can be hard to accept.

Many people attack the new year with a mission to be healthier. Giving things up is the norm when January rolls around.

Sugar? "No problem."

You can do a week of abstinence easily, a month at a push. But forever?

"No way."

"Sure, that's mad."

"Why would I?"

The changes I made happened slowly. Previously, I would have a great week and then top it off by eating and drinking crap at the weekend, allowing myself to believe that I was doing great because it was only the weekend.

Three days out of every seven is okay, isn't it?

Small steps are better than no steps.

Doing it with Fiona made it easier. We ate meals together, and cooking healthy food for two was nicer than cooking for one.

As with my exercise, I wrote down a plan. Once I knew the destination, I could build the path. The first thing I stuck on my fridge was 81kg. I was 91kg at the time. Then I wrote down how I was going to get there:

"Run/walk 3 miles, 3 nights per week (no excuses). Give up fizzy drinks."

Short and uncomplicated. And, like most things, when broken down, these goals become very doable.

What I had to do to feel good was to face reality slowly, one hurdle at a time. I learnt to mess up, accept it, and forget it. I learnt to get back on my horse and keep going. The easy option was sometimes to think, *I've screwed up my diet this week. I may as well eat and drink everything.* Sometimes, if unprepared, I'd take the easy option.

My daily eating habits are quite simple, nutritious, and delicious by this point. I have listed many of my most regular meals and snacks in the My Food Appendix. Although, a lot of these and similar recipes are available online.

Fuel for Long-term Success

The most important act in fuelling my active lifestyle is to avoid self-sabotage. For me that is basic healthy eating at home. Eating plenty of plant-based foods, drinking plenty of water, and exercising regularly. I eat fish maybe once a week and choose Irish fish, locally caught. I'm lucky enough to live by the sea, and that makes getting fresh fish easy. I shop each weekend in a local organic farmers market in Dublin's city centre. We buy all our greens for our smoothies and stock up on the everyday fruit and vegetables we need.

There are a few dishes we make every week, so we know what we need. Staying away from processed foods is easier when you're prepared. When I buy processed foods, I stick to the same formula of gluten-free, sugar-free, dairy-free food. I believe that dairy is poison and, like processed sugar, should be avoided entirely.

There are a few other ingredients that are essential to me: Rest and laughter. Of course, a good love life helps too.

If I have a doubt about food and I am in a bit of turmoil, I ask myself: Would I be comfortable giving it to my children? If the answer is no, I don't eat it. Of course, we don't live in a black-and-white world, but this is a helpful guideline. Though I gave up processed sugar a few years ago and wouldn't give it to my children, they still eat it. With all that I've read about food and diet, if I had the luxury of hiring a private chef, which I don't, I would eat a mainly raw vegan diet. As it is, I eat a lot of raw food, but at the moment, I include cooked meals each week.

If I'm training for a marathon, I do three or four runs per week totalling 40 to 50 miles. To sustain that level of activity, I will add the following into the week:

- Green smoothie—add protein and antioxidants. I use a vegan protein powder, (usually pea protein) and add spirulina powder.
- Post-run protein drink: Blend gluten-free oats, dairy-free milk (almond, oat, rice, etc.), nut butter (peanut, almond, etc.), banana, chocolate-flavoured Sunwarrior protein powder.
- When my joints start to creak and hurt, I make an anti-inflammatory drink: Hot water with apple cider vinegar, turmeric powder, cinnamon powder, cayenne pepper, fresh ginger, and a spoon of honey.
- I take 1,000 mg vitamin C daily. I choose Higher Nature True Food Vitamin C. As a child, I was anaemic, and for a period of time, had to take iron tablets daily. Now I know that's one of the first signs of being a coeliac. Vitamin C helps the absorption of iron.

As you become familiar with adding changes to your routine, allow yourself to daydream a bit. Imagine a life of improved health and wellness. What does it look like? What kinds of practices are now a part of your everyday life, and what benefits are you reaping from the work you've put in? That life is possible. You can achieve it. One powerful way of realizing the changes you wish for is to create a roadmap. The following items will lead you to permanent change. Add on to this list whatever else you like.

Roadmap to permanent change:

1. Write out your goals for the year and pin them up where you will see them every day. It's so easy to forget. You are only accountable to yourself. Don't make that option easy.

2. Clear out your cupboards of all sugar and sugar products. Sugar sucks. The only good thing about it is it sweetens food, and most of us humans love sweet. That's where it ends. Sugar calories do not fill us, and we are left feeling hungry. Next thing you know, you're eating again. Eating sugar is a cause of overeating. There are loads of sweet treats listed in the My Food Appendix.

3. Buy a NutriBullet or high-speed blender. I have a NutriBullet for small one-cup quantities and have a jug blender for bigger quantities. I waited a few years but finally got a Vitamix. They are a big investment but come with a full lifelong warranty. Once you start to drink smoothies on a regular basis, you will feel better. Once you feel better, the benefits will accrue, helping you lean towards the right choices for you. Especially around food and exercise. My "Everything Green" smoothie recipe is listed in the My Food section.

4. Read a few of the books from the My Bookshelves Appendix. If you're ready to make this change, you will be open to hearing the messages they contain. As I mentioned earlier in the book, the two that had the biggest impact on me when I started down this path were:

   The Juice Master's Ultimate Fast Food, Jason Vale

   The China Study, T. Colin Campbell

   If you still feel like this is a road you want to take, then the following big changes should appear on your list. The timeframe in which you do it is personal.

5. <u>Month one:</u> Give up sugar, fizzy drinks, and processed foods. Fizzy drinks are acidic. Too much acidity changes the body's pH levels, at which point you risk calcium and magnesium loss from bones. Consider replacing fizzy drinks with juices and smoothies.

6. <u>Month two:</u> Give up "white" everything—bread, rice, pasta. Switch to slow-releasing brown foods. This will help with energy levels and weight loss. Try brown rice, wholemeal brown pasta, and wholemeal brown bread.

7. <u>Month three:</u> Say goodbye to all forms of meat. You will reduce inflammation in your body. Your blood cholesterol levels will plummet. Your sluggish digestive system will speed up. Replace with different types of fish, Quorn, tofu, and more vegetables.

8. <u>Month four:</u> put dairy and gluten on your give-up list. Both can bloat your gut. Try alternative milks, oat, rice, soya, coconut. Hummus or coconut oil can be used as a butter replacement. Most foods are available gluten free.

9. After these changes have become the norm for you, the choice is yours as to whether you avoid them long-term or introduce them back into your diet. Whichever you choose, do it consciously.

The reason this process doesn't look easy is because it's not. It can go against the way you were raised. Sometimes it may feel like changing religion would be easier. What I can tell you is that it worked for me, and I continue to choose to eat this way daily without a feeling of sacrifice or suffering, and with joy and appreciation that I discovered a healthier lifestyle when I did.

To me, eating healthy food not only makes me feel well, but it gives me more control on my health, a bit like a safety belt.

That's how it works for me. I do believe in moderation. I also believe the best way to go is vegan. I'm not there, but I like to keep moving in that direction. Eating small amounts of meat and dairy I'm sure may work for you. Whatever you choose, know your *why*. Knowing the *why* is what gives you the determination and focus to carry you through.

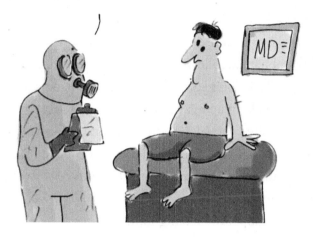

VIENNA CITY MARATHON, AUSTRIA, 23RD APRIL 2017 (MY 11TH MARATHON)

Every marathon holds a unique memory. I remember Vienna as a city of trams. Fiona, Emma, and I had arrived the previous day. The training had gone well even after I lost Emma to injury. After a seven-year sabbatical following the Rome marathon, Fiona was back to running and had entered the half marathon. Emma had booked her flights before picking up her injury, so she was going to be supporting us both. We visited the Marathon Expo and walked around the city to get our bearings. We even walked a little of the race route and took photos under the arch of the finish line. A mixture of nerves and excitement filled me. In less than 24 hours I would be crossing this line again, hopefully feeling fantastic.

Once again, all the stars aligned for a good race day. It was an early morning in April, cold, dry, and clear. I didn't know what to expect—the previous week it had been snowing. It was cold, and sun was forecast.

With 42,000 bodies racing, between the full marathon, half marathon, and the relay, the first few miles were very congested. Sometime in the first hour the sun came out, and I was too hot and sweating. I knew from experience that I'd have difficulty over the last few miles in this heat. At each water station I took a sip of water and poured the rest over my head to try and cool down. I managed to keep to my target pace of 8 minutes 45 seconds until Mile 20. Then I started to slow. I struggled to keep my time under 9 minutes per mile, and I had to dig deep.

The pain came, and I couldn't hide. I thought I couldn't bear it for another second. I tried to manage myself one step at a time. *Oh God, I thought, how could I have forgotten how bad the pain can be?*

Mile 21 was full of doubt, I tormented myself with thoughts: *Did I not drink enough? Should I have eaten during the race? Am I too old to be running a marathon?* These are three of the dozens of negative thoughts I let invade my brain.

Mile 22 I got a handle on myself and the pain, and I even felt good for a while.

Mile 23 my muscles hurt, my feet hurt, two toes on my left foot ached. I had thoughts of giving up and walking the last few miles home.

Mile 24 and, as if to accompany the pain, along came terror. Had I miscalculated my time? Was I going to break 4 hours today? This stuck with me until I crossed the finish line.

I had three goals coming into the race: My ultimate goal was a personal best, 03.51.00 or better. My second goal was under 4 hours. My third goal was to finish without injury. On my hand I had drawn a smiley face and written, "It will be worth it" in case I needed a reminder. I needed a reminder. I calculated that I had 25 minutes to go—25 minutes of this almost unbearable pain. My chest felt like it was going to explode, and my legs and feet were on fire. My head was thumping. I started to tell myself, *Run the mile you're in—only.* I repeated this over and over. I heard my friend Emma shouting, "Go on, J. You can do it." Emma should have been on this side of the barrier with me only for a knee injury. I pulled something out of the darkness to carry on. I didn't want to let Emma down, and I knew Fiona was going to pop up somewhere over the next few miles, and I really didn't want to have to face either of these fabulous women if I imploded at this stage of the race.

I still had a terrible fear that I was going to be outside of 4 hours. I fixed on a tree until I passed it, then a building, a lamp post, and so on. I knew if I just kept putting one foot in front of the other, I would eventually make it. All the while, Emma was running the last mile alongside me on the other side of the barrier. I noticed it was dense with supporters, yet she was managing to navigate her way through everyone and run faster than me.

A sign eventually appeared 500m to go. *I can do this. I can do this.* I repeated until the 400m sign appeared, followed by 300m then 200m. I could now see the finish line. I was almost home. *I could crawl across cut glass from here.*

I crossed the line in 03.51.35. That was 34 seconds slower than my best. What a mixture of feelings: total pain and elation. It would take about an hour, some food, water, and a shower before I could really celebrate in a marathon type of way. All I had to do was be present; my legs slowly lifted off the ground, and I started to float. Inner peace and satisfaction flooded all my cells. It's a hard-earned high, but it's amazing.

To my utter joy, there were showers. We were directed by German-speaking men in uniform to enter a very large military army tent. Hundreds of men were stripping naked. There was almost no light. I struggled to find a space that I could change in without bumping into too many people. I managed to take my top off, but while wrestling one of my shoes, I almost fell over and had to lean on two men to the side of me. I was in pain and cramping so badly I couldn't get to my other shoe. Another naked stranger helped me take it off. No words were spoken, just nods of understanding given. I tried to remember the spot where my bag was and moved with the flow of bodies into the next tent that had the showers. A very gentlemanly system was in order: you stepped in, showered, and stepped out. Soap was passed silently. Each man soaped outside the shower and stepped back in to rinse as another stepped out. This silent dance involved 175 to 200 naked men, rotating in semi-darkness.

Any other day this situation might have felt a bit unusual.

FOCUS

Before You Take a Step, Know Where You Want to Go

My goal is to wake up feeling fantastic, fresh, and energised by my life. That doesn't just happen by accident. I try to avoid negative people. Easier said than done. They are everywhere. I try to avoid people who don't take responsibility for themselves. I don't want life to happen to me; I want to choose it and live it. The discipline that running takes gives me a positive feeling about myself. I like myself; I couldn't always say that. It's about a lot more than putting on shoes and running; it's about self-control. To stay in on a Friday night because I have a run on Saturday morning sometimes drives my wife mad. Often it would be easier to just go out and have a few extra drinks and do the sure-life-is-too-short thing. It can be hard to strike a balance with family life and distance running.

> *If you are bored with life and you don't get up every morning*
> *with a burning desire to do things—*
> *you don't have enough goals.*
>
> Lou Holtz, American football coach

If I don't think about it, break it down, and write it, it's not a goal— it's a dream, at best, and if it's very ambitious then maybe it's just a hallucination. To make it become real, I have to see the journey. I have to focus on the details. In taking 10 minutes off a marathon time, I know that's 600 seconds faster I have to run—23 seconds per mile.

To put this in perspective, a 4-hour marathon is run at 9 minutes 9 seconds per mile. A 3-hour, 50-minute marathon is run in 8 minutes 46 seconds per mile. Once I understood what needed to be done to achieve this, I added in a speed work session one week and a hill session the following week, alternating throughout the training.

Identifying the goal is the first part of focus.

When I started, my goals were different:

- Run three miles without stopping (run a minimum of 3 nights per week)
- Enter and finish a 5k
- Lose a stone (give up processed food and sugary drinks)
- Buy a juicer and drink a vegetable juice every day

Find a Partner to Help You

After the first year of running I was feeling quite good. What now? Do I go back to Saturday mornings in bed? Friday nights out? I can tell myself, *I have ticked that box. At my age, I'm great.* But thankfully, tempting as it was, I didn't fall into that hole. I was trying to convince a friend of mine, Laura, that she should run the next Dublin marathon, and eventually she said she would, but on the condition that I ran it too. I half-heartedly agreed. I didn't take running very seriously, but we set up a training plan, put on the running shoes, and started training.

Running is, for the most part, solitary. You get to spend a lot of time facing your demons; you can even create a few new ones should you run low.

Finding a running mate was one of the most important steps for me. I started out running alone and it was hard, but probably essential for me. I would never have had a witness to the amount of huffing and puffing and sweating I had to put myself through in the first few months. Now if I don't have a training partner for a marathon, I consider skipping it. There are just too many dark, wet, cold days and nights. With five trainings per week, motivation is something I need to keep working on.

Training + Discipline = Success

There is a closeness that exists between runners. It comes from spending time together, coupled with watching each other suffer. When you go through so much together, you get insight and appreciation for what others are going through. One of the benefits of running, apart from feeling like a skinny bitch, is the people I have gotten to spend time with.

Focus is Strength

Mind over Muscle

Be it day one, month one, or year seven, keeping up with this lifestyle always takes focus. To achieve anything in life you need focus. This is something that cannot be done for you or to you.

Expectation can be a burden; misdirected focus can cripple you. For several marathons I focused on the time. Under 4 hours was the target, 03.59.59 or under, to be precise. With each attempt, the fixation on the time became an unbearable burden. The worry of not hitting my target turned into fear, a weight. During the last six miles of twenty-six, any weight is unwelcome.

In 2016 the training programme started in January and culminated in a 50k ultra in June. The Düsseldorf marathon was in April, so we treated it like a training run. Finally, I believed in the training but let go of the pressure of achieving a certain time. The result was I beat my personal record by 9 minutes! I didn't put this together until I read Matt Fitzgerald's *How Bad Do You Want It? Mastering the Psychology of Mind over Muscle.*

If this book were just about how to become a runner, I could make it a one-page book with one or two lines:

Put on your running shoes and go for a run. Repeat 3 times a week.

You are now a runner.

But this book is about more than that. My journey illustrates that everything we do or do not do in life is ruled by the choices we make. You can choose how you react to situations, positively or negatively. If you are in your fifties and want to get fit for whatever reason, the first thing you have to do is recognise your reason. Then you must choose it. You have to make that decision. You have to decide to focus. Then you have to work on improving your focus—every day.

Plans excite me; focus and clarity excite me. So much so that the "follow through" is not as mentally hard as the initial decision. Knowing myself as I do, making the right choice can be the hard part, sticking with my decision is just a formality. Not to say that it doesn't take a huge amount of work. But that is why I have to make sure I have made the right choice in the first place. There are many times in my life that I have stuck with the wrong decision, with many repercussions.

Picking a health plan demands a lot of my attention, research, and effort. At first, deciding to change something for health reasons was less complex than the new normal is to maintain. Giving up fizzy drinks, for example, took little thought and effort, yet it brought me great rewards. Today, deciding to run five marathons this year might bring me similar rewards. However, the thought and preparation are vast, not to mention the effort. Each marathon has to be planned, researched, trained for, and fuelled. (I do remind myself continuously that this is my choice, I like this me, and I appreciate feeling good and fit.) My point is, the effort it took me to focus on something small years ago is now the same effort that it takes to focus on much bigger and greater tasks.

Once a decision is made it has to be implemented, of course. For me that means no, I can't have a sneaky can of coke when I'm mad thirsty just because no one is watching. If I choose to, that's fine. But I won't pretend or bullshit myself. It takes focus and discipline, all the time. Focus also needs to be monitored and tweaked regularly. These days I'm a wannabe vegan, gluten free, and sugar free. That takes constant monitoring and discipline. However, it is all by choice, and as I see and feel the benefits, I wouldn't have it any other way. I'm three weeks into a marathon training, which means five runs a week—regardless of hail, rain, or anything else that the gods may throw at me.

Is There a Magic Pill, or Do I Have to Read This Book?

I do get asked this question a lot. The answer lies somewhere in between, depending on the type of person you are. Yes, there is a magic pill. No, I don't know if it's the red one or the blue one; and, yes, the wrong one kills you.

However, there is a magic formula: Decide where you want to be. Clarify your goal. Figure out what changes you need to apply to get there. Decide to implement these changes. Focus and act. Now your success will all hinge on your discipline. When the going gets tough, and it will, if you do not want your goal enough, you will falter. Expect as much success as you have discipline. The end.

Focus is a process that needs constant attention and tweaking. Everything changes.

Change is constant. Make sure your focus can keep up.

100KM FOREST MARATHON, PORTUMNA, GALWAY, IRELAND, 10TH JUNE 2017 (MY 12TH MARATHON)

> *Wherever you go, there you are.*
>
> Confucius

T-minus 13 ...

Thirteen days to go, and I have been panicking for over a week now. This is the longest race that I have entered so far, by thirty-one miles. A 62-mile/100km ultra. Since I booked accommodation about a week ago, I have had butterflies in my stomach. Three days ago, I had a scheduled twenty-five-mile run. Three days before that, I knocked my lower back out and had difficulty sitting down, getting up, and generally moving about. I postponed my run by a day, dosed up on painkillers, and set off. I was near Mile 5 before the pain started easing. It returned periodically over the next few hours. I figured that during the ultra there would be pain, so I may as well get used to dealing with it.

Embrace the pain; just don't mix it up with injury.

I was following my strategy: run slowly and walk the big hills. I had never walked during a run before and found this very hard. I keep worrying I might not be able to start again. Today every second thought seems to be, *Oh my God, what am I doing?* or something a bit less printable. I have been very nervous.

T-minus 12 …

I sent a text to my sports psychologist friend, Neil O'Brien, and explained what I am planning to do and asked, "What can I do?" He replied, "Don't do it." Probably good advice.

But I can't help thinking, *I can't fail now—I've trained for five months. I'm fit, I'm strong, and I feel healthy. Whatever happens will happen.* If nothing else, the success is the five months of training. I have had a great year so far, and it's only May. I feel fantastic, I feel fit, I feel strong, and I am at my target weight of 79kg. The cut-off time for the race is 15 hours. If I make it over the line with one second to go, that will be a success—after all, it's my first 100k. If I don't make it, I'll just have to come back next year. How bad?

I know that's all true, I'd just like to be feeling it a bit more.

I feel a bit better now; maybe I should focus on some of the fun. Maybe I should give some thought to food and supplies.

T-minus 6 …

I'm not sleeping great. I'm tired. I'm nervous. All the things I've read about ultrarunning have morphed into one: "90% is in your head, the other 10% is mental." Is there any truth in that, or is it just a funny saying? How can I possibly know how I'm going to react in my head when I hit Mile 40 or 50? What will happen? Will I start getting strange thoughts? Ticked that box long ago. Will my leg fall off? I know from marathons that I have been in a terrible state on occasions, suffered blinding pain that made me want to quit. Yet it was always temporary, otherwise I wouldn't be in this predicament right now. What will I face in this race that I have never had to face before?

I'm scared. Scared that I will fail. Scared I won't make it in under 15 hours. I think I need to believe that I can do it. I can remember how good it felt last year at the 50k/31-mile finish line. The last three miles were particularly painful. My kidneys and stomach ached as did my lungs, head, knees, feet, and toes. Yet after I went through the finish line, the pain disappeared. (I had stopped running, of course.)

When I lose focus how will I get back? I know, where focus goes, energy flows, and if my focus goes to how badly I feel, my energy will follow and give the negative thoughts and feelings power. It's not possible to focus for 13 or 14 hours, so I will have to work on getting back into the zone when I fall out.

T-minus 5 ...

I don't have to run this race. I'm running it because I want to. I chose this. This is the juice for me. These days of nerves are what I asked for. This excitement is the best. Suck it up!

I must leave my ego at home. I will look like shit and feel like shit. I just have to hold it together when the wheels fall off. I think I'm going to find out what I'm made of on Saturday.

T-minus 4 ...

Whatever happens may stay with me for a long time. If I slip up and become a DNF (Did Not Finish) it will live with me and become part of me, maybe forever. I don't want that inside me. If I give everything and come up short, that might be different. As long as I have given my all—mentally and physically—I should be okay. What more can I do? I know the mind controls the body, so if I can spend the day focusing on positivity and composure, I should be good. I hope so. I'm going to see just how strong I am. I think I'm going to meet the real me on Saturday. What a prospect.

T-minus 3 …

I'm feeling calm today, I didn't sleep much, but I think I have a handle on my head. I have been visualising myself running from Mile 50 to Mile 60. It's hard, and it's incredibly painful, but I can cope. If I could start right now, I would. The wait is tough. I'm not sure how long I can keep up this calm. There was a time when I felt this nervous about the Rathfarnham 5k race. That thought gives me comfort.

T-minus 1 …

One more sleep. Time to pack. Weather forecast for Galway tomorrow is 18C, dry and sunny. Two pairs of running shoes, several tops, two pairs of socks, shorts, first aid kit, sunglasses, sunscreen, food, breakfast, Vaseline, salt tablets, waterproofs, lunch and dinner that I can digest when running. I think I have everything covered. I will go for a few easy miles this afternoon before heading to Galway. The fat lady's starting to sing.

Portumna Forest Marathon 100k

At 03.45 I got up and put on some porridge. I want to have eaten 3 hours before the starting gun. One hell of a storm was banging about outside. I figured I'd start in my heavy waterproof trail runners. If the day cleared up, I'd switch to the lighter Hoka One One's. I tried desperately to focus on the next 13 hours.

Head checklist:

- It's only a run. Don't waste energy. Don't panic.
- When the time comes, separate pain from injury.
- 20 laps of 5 kilometres—run the laps, not the kilometres.
- Focus on the positive.
- Believe.

Bang! And we were off.

One hundred running the 50k, and fifty the 100k.

The relief of movement.

On that first lap, the chatty chatted, the silent—like myself—remained silent. There would be plenty of time for getting to know each other. I moved in as fluid a state as I could, relaxing my muscles and joints. I figured I was in good shape, no unusual aches or pains. The day was looking good.

Five laps later, fifteen miles in, the storm was long over, and the temperature had risen to 20C. Sweat was something I needed to keep an eye on; dehydration could be an issue even on a cold day. I had a mouthful of water every two and a half miles. The line between too much and too little is a tough one. Too much and the stomach cramps, too little and your day could be over very early.

Lap 9 came and went. Mile 30 was coming up soon, and I figured twenty-three more miles before I got to the business end of this race. *Just keep running at the same pace. Body check, energy levels good, calves, knees, hamstrings all good.*

Mile 40 came, and I was in lap 14, tired and melting from the sun, but I felt good. I had never run this far, but I had broken the back of this one. That thought made me feel good. I was starting to notice others that had maybe started out too fast or taken too much or too little food. Some were in distress.

Mile 50 came, and I felt like banging my chest and screaming, "I'm still here." Only I didn't need to. I would only have been shouting it at myself, and I was only too aware. Twelve miles left was four laps. Four out of twenty, I knew then I had this beat. For the first time I started to enjoy myself.

I introduced myself to other runners that I hadn't spoken to and became very aware of my surroundings. Portumna Forest Park is very green. There is a section that runs beside the lake and a strong cool wind was blowing in. The sheer joy of a cool breeze was the first wonderful thing I had felt in a while. Another runner called out, "We'll all enjoy a cold beer tonight." Now I felt comfortable enough to smile and let my thoughts go to the end of the race.

At Mile 51 I hit an "Oh God, I can't go on," spell. With eleven miles to go, I felt in a very lonely place. I concentrated on where I was at that very moment. I kept that in-the-moment feeling and consciously moved my legs forward. I paid attention to the trees and the birds. I marvelled at how carefree the birds seemed. I imagined the life of a tree. Eventually I came back and was okay again.

The last three miles were not much different than the previous thirty. The panic and pain I had anticipated never materialised. I never got to meet that real me I had been preparing for. I think I was too well trained for panic and pain. Crossing the finish line was an incredible experience. The work I had put into this race, the amount of thought I had put into this. The nights I lay awake worrying that I might not have had what it takes to finish. The word satisfaction took on a new meaning.

My limits were all in my head, as expected. Do we spend our lives in our comfortable box?

There was a time I would have given anything to be able to run around the block without stopping. I grew to running a 5k without needing a day off work. Then on to a half marathon then a full.

I had just run sixty-two miles. What's next?

Later I had a beer. The man had been right—it was incredible.

COGNITIVE DISSONANCE

When you want to succeed as bad as you want to breathe
then you'll be successful.

Eric Thomas

Nothing Changes until You Do

There is an obstacle we often place in front of ourselves when it comes to achieving something. Sometimes we just talk ourselves out of things to avoid an internal conflict. For example, if we hold a belief that we should not add to polluting the environment, yet we purchase a car that is very heavy on emissions, we either decide that we don't care about the environment or we plan to cycle to work a few days a week.

A person who experiences inconsistency tends to become psychologically uncomfortable, and so is motivated to try and reduce the cognitive dissonance recurring by actively avoiding situations and information likely to increase the psychological discomfort. Many religious people in my life come to mind. They refuse to hear anything that causes an internal conflict—like, say, science.

What we see depends mainly on what we look for.

John Lubbock

Many of us are addicted to food—often food that is damaging to us. Yet we are masters at hiding our habit from ourselves. We will often focus on the good meals we eat and totally block out the junk snacks and drinks we consume when no one is looking.

We regularly monitor our exercise all the time and our diet some of the time. Our addictions—perceived or otherwise—to sugar, trans fats, and animal products somehow change our views on food rather than make us face a few truths.

The other side of fear is life.

Before I go on a rant, I want to preface the next paragraph with "in my experience." I'm not a psychologist, but I can't ignore the number of us who are struggling. A lot of us eat to fill a void we don't even know we have, and until we can face that demon, no diet or positive exercise is going to help. We may pick a new diet plan, stick to it rigidly, and lose, say 10kg. Yet unless we face and deal with the demon that we are hiding from, we will bounce right back to where we were.

We don't all try and eat our problems. Some of us drink them. Others of us go to sex, drugs, gambling, and God knows what else. Yet the outcome is the same: if we don't face our shit, it comes right back at us. When we don't face what's in our closet, our feelings of self-worth are so poor that we can be more comfortable at the bottom of the ladder. I think the first step is to recognise the problem.

If you can't get rid of the skeleton in your closet, you'd best teach it to dance.

George Bernard Shaw

Eating animal products is another example. Despite the evidence that red meat and dairy are bad for human health, most of us choose to ignore it. Rather than take this on board and cut back on animal products, we often choose to fight this view.

My mother always served us meat and milk, so why shouldn't I eat it and serve it to my children?

My granny drank milk every day and lived to ninety.

Sure, life is too short!

We choose to ignore all the evidence that shows animal products are bad for us, often by refusing to read any articles or books that support this view. We even love our dog and think we are animal lovers, yet we happily eat every other animal we can sink our teeth into, refusing to see the cruelty and torture we inflict. Not to mention the environmental shitstorm we cause by eating red meat. A friend of mine would think nothing of buying several bags of bird food every week during winter to make sure the birds in his neighbourhood don't suffer, yet he would sit by his window looking at the birds feeding while munching on the leg of a chicken.

Eating meat is a personal choice. Eating a plant-based diet works for me. I started doing it for health reasons. I never gave a thought for animals. Over time my thoughts have changed. Now I think if I can live a healthy life without harming others, why wouldn't I?

What about you? Where does the dissonance niggle at your consciousness? Do you ignore it, fight it, and push it away? Try listening sometime. Engage those thoughts. You might be surprised where they lead you.

EXERCISING WOULD BE SO
MUCH MORE REWARDING IF
YOUR CALORIES SCREAMED
WHILE YOU BURNED THEM

LAST ONE STANDING, ENNISKILLEN, FERMANAGH, NORTHERN IRELAND, 19TH AUGUST 2017 (MY 13TH MARATHON)

One of the ways I pick a race is by the level of fear or excitement it instils in me. While running the Portumna 100k, I was talking to a guy named Mark (now a friend of mine), and he asked me if I wanted to take part in the Enniskillen Last One Standing race two months later. The course is a 4.2-mile loop on trail. Runners have one hour to complete the first loop and be at the starting line ready to go again at the top of the hour. This repeats every hour until there is only one left standing.

I said, "No, you freak. That sort of race wouldn't interest me." A few days later I was still thinking about it. Two weeks later I realised that every time it crossed my mind, I felt a mixture of fear and excitement.

Fiona said, "Why don't you enter that Last One Standing race?"

I said, "Why don't you?"

She laughed and said, "That race was made for you."

A week later I entered.

This race was clearly out of my comfort zone. The Last One Standing Ultra is unique in that there is no set distance. Runners start around the 4.2-mile loop at noon. They start again on the hour, every hour, until there is only one participant left. If you are back at the starting line in time, you go again. If not, you are disqualified. To rest you must run faster. Every hour everyone is equal again. It's brutal, and it's relentless, and the mental and physical fatigue builds. Not knowing where the finish line is can play with your head. The previous year had taken 36 hours to reveal a winner. What could go wrong?

The night before, Fiona and I spent most of the evening making soup and preparing food. I had discovered the joy of soup during the Portumna 100km Ultra earlier in the year. As a coeliac, I regularly have difficulty eating and running, but I learned soup was something I could digest without discomfort. We got up with the sun and headed north.

At midday in picturesque Enniskillen, Co Fermanagh, the hooter sounded for lap 1, and we were off. It resembled a horn from *The Lord of the Rings*, calling the Orcs to attack. Maybe that was a sign right there. It was a beautiful route through woods and countryside. I was immediately worried at the amount of uphill terrain. It was not a problem in the beginning, but I feared it might soon be. There was fun and laughter, and with only forty-nine runners it felt very social. I started with a friend, and we made it back in 45 minutes. Way too fast, we made a note to complete the next lap 5 minutes slower.

Laps 2, 3, and 4 were a case of going through the motions and enjoying the scenery. I got to meet many runners and heard some unusual stories.

On lap 5 and heading for the 20.2-mile point, the chats thinned out, and the participants started to drop. I could feel the race was now *on*.

The miles passed slowly, and darkness came. Around Mile 30, I could feel my body struggling. The woods became eerie. Had zombies appeared, they wouldn't have been out of place. *Best to keep moving*, I thought.

On hour ten, Mile 40, I was in trouble. I was falling apart. All the positive quotes and sayings I had written down counted for nothing now. I was past it. My legs hurt, my lungs were contracting, and I had difficulty catching a full breath. My kidneys hurt. It was all pain now. Resistance was futile.

I had become one of the zombies.

Dropping in the woods held no fear for me now. Before the race, I had asked Fiona to make sure I started the next lap if I wanted to quit. Being timed out and disqualified is very different to giving up.

As I lay over a table trying to convince my body to get back up, my wife, Fiona, said, "You know you're going back out."

I said, "No, I am not. I can't."

"Yes, you are," she said.

"I don't think I can stand without throwing up."

"Whatever. You're still going back out," she said.

At the start line, I couldn't stand without holding on. I had to keep moving. Forwards, sideways, just to stay upright. About a third of the way around the loop, there is a waterfall with a bank and a drop of about eight or ten feet. I thought if I fell in, I would do some damage but probably live. I decided to "accidentally" fall in when I got there. In total darkness with only the narrow beam of light attached to my forehead, I missed it. After the race, Fiona said she hadn't been sure I would make it back from that loop.

Running alone in the woods, in the dark, in pain, is an experience. My thoughts flowed and jumped unchecked. My energy tanks were empty. My sane mind left me, and my demons moved in. Two laps later, I finished the loop 2 minutes and 30 seconds late. At 3 minutes past midnight, 12 hours, 2 minutes and 30 seconds in, and 50.4 miles from the starting point, I was disqualified.

My night was over.

The hardest race I had ever run or even imagined was over. I had nothing left.

"Don't worry. You'll do better next year," was said as a DNF (Did Not Finish) medal was put around my neck.

"No, I won't," I said. "I won't ever be back here."

I didn't even know what day it was. I felt fucked, three ways from Sunday. It took 26 hours for all but one runner to drop out. On loop 27 there was a winner.

I learnt something in Enniskillen I immediately knew would stand to me later on: if you allow your focus to drop, your demons will eat you alive.

It took three days for thoughts to sneak back in, like, *If I trained better next year, I could do better.* I thought, *Next year I'm going to make the 100 miles if it kills me.*

One part of me is afraid it might.

RACING

British Bulldogs

There was a time when I wouldn't run around the block to save my life. I don't know why. I think it was because sports were always easy for me when I was in school. I also never liked doing anything if I couldn't see the point. In school I played rugby, and I loved it. The school I attended was located on the side of a mountain in a place called Rathfarnham, and on Wednesdays, cross-country running was obligatory. I tried hard, but I couldn't get my head around it. What was the point? Where was the sport? When I was in junior school, at break time we would play British Bulldogs. Everyone would line against a wall and charge to a facing wall. One lone kid had to stand in the middle and force another to the ground. Once you hit the ground, you became one of the those in the middle. Eventually, everyone was stopped. To be the last one wrestled to the ground gave you great standing. I totally got that. Cross-country running was absolutely lost on me. As a result, I never did it, not once. I would take detention before I would run around aimlessly. Now it's called trail running and I pay to do it. How things change.

My first running race was a 5k. I was forty-five and still thought of myself as fit and strong. The twenty-year gap in exercise should have sent up a flag, but it didn't. I huffed, puffed, wobbled, and staggered my way over the finish line. That day I got the nickname "Wounded Bear."

I evolved, and as I trained for the next race, the difference was phenomenal. I set a target, and I had the discipline to train for it. The satisfaction to notice your shortcomings, work hard at rectifying them, and complete a race in your target zone is hard to match.

Over time, as you know by now, I moved to marathons. A marathon is so hard and far that I always thought we deserved to run it abroad, where possible, preferably in a city we had never been in before.

I stick by this philosophy, and it serves me well. I get to visit a lot of places I would not have reason to visit otherwise. Each marathon gives me months of excitement. Getting the training right, and eating and sleeping right are all factors. I love that each run forces me to be healthy. Without a race in sight, I find it hard to motivate myself to exercise to the degree that it's beneficial. Going to bed early on a Friday night is not going to happen without a race looming.

When I entered my first marathon, I thought that would be it. But the lifestyle is addictive. My first 50k was scary. My first 100k was terrifying. After each challenge my boundaries shift. The impossible becomes possible. I get excited by events that, a few years previously, I thought were reserved for those with a loose connection. I now know that once you believe something, it's possible.

As I mentioned near the beginning of the book, some of my habits have changed. *The Big Book of Endurance Training and Racing* by Dr. Philip Maffetone changed my behaviour around racing. He taught me to run on fat, not sugar. When I wanted to run ultra marathons, I needed to fuel my runs more efficiently. The first step of running on fat is to give up sugar. Years on and even in my day-to-day life I feel better for this.

Giving up dairy was maybe my greatest discovery. It wasn't until I took the step of cutting it from my diet that I realised how much it affects my breathing. At first, I thought I was being crippled with a head cold. Whenever I need nutrition advice, I turn to my sister Sarah. I told her about my blocked-up head. She laughed and advised me that it was not a head cold, but my body expelling all the toxins I had been pumping in with dairy. Three weeks later I could breathe and speak—I could also hear better and taste better. I could run farther and for longer. Training my legs to carry me short, average, or even great distances is minor compared to training my lungs. Now if I eat dairy, I notice the difference it makes to my breathing within minutes.

Fuelling for a race is very personal and different for everyone. My routine consists of gluten-free porridge 3 hours before a race. Nothing during, except water. This applies to races up to 42km. Anything over and I have to think about what I can eat that will digest quickly, without pain, while running. So far, through trial and a lot of error, I am good with vegetable soup. And sometimes peanut butter. I watch other competitors eating pizza and sandwiches and I look on with a bit of envy.

The downside of eating food that doesn't agree with you while running is great. Cramps and digestion pains can ruin any run. Not to mention vomiting and diarrhoea. Even too much water sloshing around your stomach can be miserable.

WITH ALL DUE
RESPECT, IF YOU'RE
NOT A DISTANCE
RUNNER I DISCREDIT
YOUR DEFINITION
OF **TIRED**

MOSCOW MARATHON, RUSSIA, 24TH SEPTEMBER 2017 (MY 15TH MARATHON)

As the connecting flight leaves Frankfurt and heads to Moscow, my thoughts and feelings are about fifty miles ahead of the plane. Once again I tell myself, this is the juice. The butterflies make me jittery and nervous. I love this feeling. Fiona is reading a Moscow guide aloud—reminding me that there is life outside marathons. There are cafés, bars, restaurants, museums, and tourist attractions everywhere. Even the underground Metro that takes you around is spectacular. Apparently. According to this guide, four nights might not be enough.

We've never been to Moscow before. Our Russian is limited. I have three words, four at a push. Fiona has a grasp on the alphabet and a few phrases, so if we hang together, I should be okay.

Running marathons has taken me to places I might not have otherwise had reason to visit. Armagh City in Northern Ireland was my last, a city with a population of 15,000. Today a city of 14.2 million.

After I put my first foot into the underground Metro, I knew that I was stepping into something special. Having visited London many times and lived in New York, I have seen subways before. But I have never seen anything like the Moscow Metro. With nine million journeys taken every day, it is clearly a functioning underground system. That's more than New York and London combined. Over the next 4 days, 90 seconds was the longest we waited for a train. Someone told me they once had to wait 3 minutes. Two other things struck me: the friendliness of the people and the cleanliness of the city.

It must be a cultural value, I thought, after another notable difference I observed just before the race. At the beginning of every marathon at least 20% of the runners have to pee. It's a nerves thing. In Rome hundreds of men and women lined the grassy banks on the sides of the starting corrals, squeezing out one last pee. Every city I have run in I have experienced something similar. But not Moscow. I did not see one person head for the bushes. On Mile 13, I ran by three port-a-loos, each with a long queue. There were two military men standing close by. The surrounding bushes remained untouched. I thought I had seen law abiding in Germany, but this was a new level. Maybe they know something about the military that I don't. I didn't even see anyone jaywalking.

My greatest surprise was that Moscow is so full of colour. In all the Cold War movies, the city looks so cold and dour. Always black and white with a heavy dose of grey. And now the sun shone and the sky was blue.

On marathon day it was sweltering hot, without a cloud in the sky. This was going to be a problem. I decided to run to enjoy, and not to try and break any records. I didn't really have a choice. We arrived early as advised, to get through security. Fiona and I wished each other good luck and went to our starting areas.

As we were corralled into our starting blocks, five drones criss-crossed each other, videoing the runners from above our heads while we waited to start. The hooter went and, as always, the release of tension that comes with movement was wonderful. The first water station 5k in came not a second too soon. I drank a cup of water, poured one on my head, and tucked a wet sponge into my shirt at the back of my neck. I did the same every 5k for the rest of the race. The heat was intense, and every time I had a strong thirst before I got close to the next water station.

Having spent the previous day sightseeing, it was great to recognise some areas. Somehow it makes the distance shorter. By the time we hit the Kremlin, about eighteen miles in, my muscles were starting to cramp. This had never happened to me before. I had to slow down. I walked Mile 25 to 26 with great difficulty. I just about managed to run the last few hundred metres.

After finishing, I collected my medal and sat in the stand set up at the finish, watching runners crossing the finish line. I remembered starting out eight years ago. I thought about the cold nights struggling around Dublin. I laughed to myself at how far out of my comfort zone I had ventured. I had just run my fifteenth marathon, and I was sitting at the finish line in Moscow feeling a little smug. I was trying to spot Fiona running through the finish, when I passed out. I woke a few moments later. I think a woman woke me and offered me a banana. I got up and thanked her, took the banana, and moved out of the stand. There is safety at ground level. I felt weak and had to struggle not to throw up. I went in and out of sleep and sweats for a while before regaining my composure. I thought, *When is this shit going to get easier?* I put it down to the heat, general tiredness, and exhaustion. Whatever it was, lying on the side of the road, semi-conscious, trying not to throw up was not how I saw this going.

Half an hour later, after a lot of water and a few bananas, I had mostly recovered. My bad spell had passed, and now I felt very alive.

When Fiona crossed the finish line, she looked so well and fresh, and had a big smile. It reminded me that being fit and healthy is streets ahead of being competitive. Moderation is where it's at. As if I needed a reminder. Having to run farther, faster, is very personal and probably not recommended.

I thought, *Next time I run a race it will be at a relaxed pace, and I will finish with a smile looking fresh.* Even I knew the thought was a lie.

Fiona and I headed back to the hotel and slept for an hour.

Then we headed out to celebrate.

APPENDIXES

When I read health and fitness books, there are a few bits I go back to again and again, usually training plans, recipes, and tips. I've put all those bits together in the following appendixes.

Appendix A: My Food

Appendix B: My Marathons and Ultramarathons

Appendix C: My Bookshelves (and Other Favourites)

Appendix D: My Training Plans

APPENDIX A:

MY FOOD

This appendix contains a sample of meals I like and eat regularly. First, though, a few of my basic guidelines:

- Sea salt + rock salt only. Dump table salt.
- White is out. I try to stick to the "white is shite" rule, and I never go far wrong. No white pasta, bread, or rice. I buy dairy-, sugar-, and gluten-free brown bread from Kim at my local Saturday farmers market. If you're not lucky enough to have a Kim of your own, try and source something homemade locally.
- Avoid all fizzy drinks (i.e., Diet Coke, sugar-free flavoured water, Red Bull, etc.).
- Drink a minimum of 2 litres of water per day.
- Replace butter with coconut oil.
- Use coconut oil for cooking, and keep olive oil for salad dressing. I never use liquid oils for frying or baking—always coconut oil.
- Replace milk with almond, oat, or soya milk—always unsweetened.
- Avoid processed food. If eating takeout, choose Indian, Thai, or Japanese. (Ask for dishes to be prepared dairy free. They will use coconut milk instead.) Chinese often contains monosodium glutamate (MSG). This is used as a flavour enhancer. It is also pasted onto food to give it a shine, giving it a fresher, more appealing look. For decades it has been linked to various health problems such as headaches, bloating, and allergic reactions.
- Avoid all sugar. Read every label. (You will get used to it and become a speed-reader from 10 metres.) Sugar will regularly be listed more than once in an ingredients list to disguise it. If required, sweeten with honey.

48 common aliases for sugar:

- Barley malt
- Beet sugar
- Brown sugar
- Buttered syrup crystals
- Cane sugar
- Caramel
- Carob syrup
- Castor sugar
- Corn syrup
- Corn syrup solids
- Confectioner's sugar
- Date sugar
- Demerara sugar
- Dextran
- Dextrose
- Diastase
- Diastatic malt
- Ethyl maltol
- Fructose
- Fruit juice
- Fruit juice concentrate
- Galactose
- Glucose
- Glucose solids
- Golden sugar
- Golden syrup
- Grape sugar

- High-fructose corn syrup
- Honey
- Icing sugar
- Invert sugar
- Lactose
- Maltodextrin
- Maltose
- Malt syrup
- Maple syrup
- Molasses
- Muscovado sugar
- Panocha
- Raw sugar
- Refiners syrup
- Rice syrup
- Sorbitol
- Sorghum syrup
- Sucrose sugar
- Treacle
- Turbinado sugar
- Yellow sugar

RECIPES

These recipes are simple and easy to make. They've also been tried and tested by me. I've listed *"Books That Gave Me New Ways to Prepare Food"* in Appendix C. Without these chefs and cooks, I wouldn't have as much delicious food to eat. If I had to pick just one book for getting started, it would probably be *The Happy Pear: Recipes and Stories from the First Ten Years*. It has lots of tips and easy recipes.

If you need a starting place, maybe start by replacing your cornflakes and milk then slowly work your way through the rest!

Breakfast

Porridge

(gf) with water, almond, soya, or oat milk[3]

Add seeds, raisins, goji berries, cinnamon, and sea salt. I add anything that takes my eye, nuts and fruit being two favourites. This is a filling and inexpensive dish.

Granola

- 500 g gluten-free porridge oats
- 500 g mixed nuts (almonds, hazelnuts, pecan—or whatever you have on hand)
- 200 g mixed seeds (sunflower, sesame, pumpkin—or whatever you have on hand)
- 2 tablespoons honey
- ½ teaspoon cinnamon
- Big pinch salt
- 1 teaspoon vanilla extract
- ½ cup coconut oil

---

3 Most oat milks are not gluten free, so keep an eye on the label if you are coeliac.

After toasting:

200 g dried fruits (goji berries, dates, raisins, apricots, figs—or whatever you have on hand)

Heat the oven to a moderate temperature: 180C/fan 160C/gas mark 4.

Put all the oats, nuts, and seeds in a large ovenproof dish.

Put the honey, cinnamon, salt, vanilla, and coconut oil on top.

Don't bother melting the coconut oil. After a few minutes in the oven it will have melted.

Put the dish in the oven.

Every 15 minutes take the dish out of the oven and give it a good mix.

Keep a close eye on it; the granola is ready when the oats have toasted golden brown.

Take out of the oven and allow to cool.

Once it's cool, you can add the dried fruits to the mix (if adding larger fruits like dates or figs, chop them into smaller chunks before adding).

Store in an airtight container.

Serve with almond, soya, or oat milk.

Vegan Pancakes

- 3 cups gluten-free rolled oats or oat flour[4]
- 2 cups almond milk
- ½ teaspoon cinnamon
- ¼ teaspoon vanilla bean powder or extract
- ½ cup of blueberries or chopped strawberries is nice to add to the batter before you fry them

I like to have lots of topping choices on the table when I serve these.

I usually include:

- Avocado
- Banana
- Peanut or almond butter
- Maple syrup or honey
- Berries
- Coconut yogurt

Place oats in a high-speed blender and process until a flour is reached.

Add milk, cinnamon, and vanilla; mix until batter is formed.

Stir in the blueberries or strawberries.

Heat in a non-stick pan on medium and pour ⅓ cup of batter, using a measuring cup to ensure equal size and cooking times.

Serve with your choice of toppings.

---

4 Oat flour can be replaced with gluten-free self-raising flour.

Soups

Sweet Potato & Chestnut Mushroom Soup

- 2 red onions, chopped
- 2 cloves of garlic, chopped
- 2 carrots, sliced
- 2 sweet potatoes, sliced
- 1 stick of celery, sliced
- 150 g chestnut mushrooms, sliced
- 2 tablespoons coconut oil
- 6 sprigs of fresh thyme
- 60 ml red wine
- 2.5 litres vegetable stock or water
- 1 tablespoon tamari or soy sauce
- Salt and freshly ground black pepper

Peel and chop the red onions and garlic. Finely slice the carrots, sweet potatoes, celery, and mushrooms.

Heat the oil in a large family size pan on a low to medium heat. Add the onions and the sprigs of thyme and cook gently for 3 minutes. Add the red wine and allow to cook for another 3 minutes. Now add the garlic, carrots, and celery and cook for a further 5 minutes. Add the sweet potato and mushrooms and cook for a further 10 minutes, stirring regularly.

Add the stock and tamari and bring to the boil. Reduce the heat and simmer for 15 minutes, until the veg are fully cooked. Remove the sprigs of thyme and blend the soup with a stick blender.

Taste and season with salt and black pepper before serving.

Pea & Parsley Soup

- 1 tablespoon coconut oil
- 1 medium onion, finely chopped
- A few sprigs of thyme, leaves only, chopped
- 1 litre vegetable stock
- 500 g fresh shelled peas or frozen peas
- 20 g flat leaf parsley, chopped
- Sea salt and freshly ground pepper to taste
- A few mint leaves shredded to finish (optional) and some olive oil to drizzle

Heat the oil in a large saucepan over a medium-low heat and sweat the onion with the thyme until soft and translucent, about 10 minutes.

Add the stock, peas (reserving a handful to finish the soup if you like), and parsley. Season with salt and pepper, bring to simmer and cook for 5–10 minutes or until peas are very tender.

Allow to cool slightly then puree the soup in a food processor or blender, or with a stick blender, until very smooth. Return the soup to the pan; adjust the seasoning and reheat.

Ladle the soup into warmed bowls. If you have some fresh peas scatter on the top. Add the mint. Trickle a little olive oil or rapeseed oil on top and serve.

Alternatively, you can let the soup go cold then chill it slightly before serving. Add the scattering of peas and mint and, if using, the trickle of oil at the last minute.

<u>Salads</u>

Chickpea & Squash Salad

- 130 g of butternut squash, peeled and cut into bite-sized chunks
- 1 teaspoon paprika
- 1 teaspoon dried mixed herbs
- Salt and pepper
- Coconut oil
- 80 g chickpeas, drained and rinsed
- ½ teaspoon chilli powder
- Handful of rocket
- 40 g sun-dried tomatoes, chopped

Dressing:

- 1 tablespoon olive oil
- ½ tablespoon apple cider vinegar
- ½ teaspoon turmeric
- 1 teaspoon honey

Preheat the oven to 220C/fan 200C.

Peel the squash then cut it into small bite-sized pieces. Place on a baking tray with the paprika, mixed herbs, and a little salt and coconut oil. Bake for about 30 minutes until tender.

Place the chickpeas on a separate baking tray with the chilli powder, toss well to coat, and bake for 20 minutes until they are firm but not too crunchy.

Mix all the dressing ingredients together, seasoning with a bit of salt and lots of pepper.

Once the chickpeas and the squash have cooked and cooled, mix them with the rocket and sun-dried tomatoes, then pour on the dressing and toss everything.

Works just as well with sweet potato instead of squash.

Kale, Sprouted Beans, & Goji Salad

I just love this. When mixing the dressing with the salad by hand, I find it impossible not to lick my fingers clean after.

A total superfood that tastes fantastic. This is a seriously high anti-oxidant-rich salad.

- 400 g kale
- 3 pinches salt
- 1 teaspoon lemon juice
- 3 teaspoons extra virgin olive oil
- 200 g sprouted bean mix
- 100 g sunflower seeds
- 100 g goji berries

Dressing:

- 1 clove of garlic
- 125 ml tahini
- 80 g cashew nuts
- 1 tablespoon lemon juice
- ½ teaspoon salt
- 2 teaspoons of honey or maple syrup
- 1 teaspoon ground coriander
- 1 teaspoon ground cumin
- 1 teaspoon paprika
- ¼ teaspoon chilli powder
- 2 tablespoons extra virgin olive oil

Remove the kale leaves from the stalks. Chop the leaves roughly with a scissors and wash well then put them in a large bowl. Add the salt, lemon juice, and olive oil and massage the kale leaves with your hands for 2 minutes. The kale will turn a darker green and will soften.

Wash the sprouted beans and drain well. Toast the sunflower seeds in a dry frying pan over a medium heat for a few minutes until they start to brown.

Peel the garlic then put into a high-speed blender with the rest of the dressing ingredients and blend until smooth. If you don't have a high-speed blender, use a food processor. You may need to add water to the dressing to loosen it, though it should still be thick.

Add the dressing to the bowl of kale and mix really well. Then stir in the sprouted beans, goji berries, and toasted sunflower seeds.

Beetroot with Walnut & Cumin

This is to die for! A real treat.

- 75 g walnuts
- 1 teaspoon cumin seeds
- 400 g beetroot
- A good handful of parsley, chopped
- Juice of a small orange
- 1 squeeze of lemon juice
- 1 tablespoon rapeseed oil
- Sea salt and freshly ground black pepper

To finish (optional):

- 2 tablespoons plain dairy-free, unsweetened yogurt (coconut or soya are good)
- More toasted and roughly bashed cumin
- A pinch of hot smoked paprika

Heat a frying pan over a medium heat and add the walnuts. Toast gently for a few minutes, tossing often, until they smell toasted and are colouring in a few places. Tip into a mortar. Put the cumin seeds into the frying pan and toast gently for 1–2 minutes, tossing a few times, just until they start to release their scent. Tip onto a plate to stop cooking further.

Peel the beetroot and grate it coarsely into a bowl. Add the parsley, orange juice, a squeeze of lemon juice, rapeseed oil, and some salt and pepper. Give it a good mix, taste, and adjust with seasoning. Ideally leave for 20 minutes or so—the dressing will lightly marinate and tenderise the beetroot.

Spread the beetroot in a dish or on a plate. Bash the walnuts roughly with the pestle and mortar and scatter over the beetroot. Tip the cumin seeds into the mortar and give them a rough bashing too, then scatter over the salad.

Finish with another trickle of rapeseed oil and, if you like, dot with blobs of yogurt, sprinkling with more cumin and a pinch of paprika.

Main Meals

Roast Squash & Pineapple Massaman Curry

This is a deliciously scrumptious curry—worth the trouble.

- 1 butternut squash, peeled and cut into bite-sized chunks
- 2 tablespoons coconut oil
- 250 g pineapple chunks
- 1 clove garlic, crushed
- 1 white onion, chopped
- 2 x 400 ml cans of coconut milk
- 1 tablespoon tamarind paste
- 2 star anise
- 1 teaspoon ground turmeric
- 1 teaspoon ground coriander
- 1 teaspoon ground cardamom
- Pinch of ground cloves
- Pinch of grated nutmeg
- Pinch of ground cinnamon
- 1 tablespoon tamari (gluten-free soy sauce)
- 1 tablespoon manuka honey
- 4 spring onions, chopped
- 100 g green beans, trimmed
- 50 g cashew nuts
- Juice of 1 lime
- Handful of coriander leaves to garnish
- Steamed brown rice to serve

Preheat the oven to 180C/fan 160C/gas mark 4.

Slice the squash in half and scoop out the seeds. Cut the flesh into chunks and add to a large roasting tray with one tablespoon of coconut oil. Once it has been in the oven a few minutes, the coconut oil will have melted. Give the squash a quick mix to spread oil throughout.

Add the pineapple chunks to the roasting tray and turn up the oven to 220C/fan 200C/gas mark 7. Roast for a further 10 minutes until lightly brown and tender. Meanwhile, heat the rest of the coconut oil in a large saucepan. Fry the garlic and onion for 5 minutes until softened. Add the coconut milk and stir in the tamarind paste, spices, tamari, and honey. Simmer for 10 minutes until the spices and tamarind are fully absorbed.

Add the roast squash and pineapple, the green beans, spring onions, cashews, and half the lime juice to the pan and simmer for a further 5–10 minutes.

Serve warm, sprinkled with coriander leaves, add the remaining lime juice, alongside a bowl of steamed brown rice.

The spices in this dish possess healing potential: cardamom is an antioxidant and removes toxins from the body, and turmeric and coriander are strong anti-inflammatories.

Pumpkin Curry with Chickpeas

A super-easy and tasty curry.

- 1 tablespoon coconut oil
- 3 tablespoon Thai yellow curry paste, or vegetarian alternative
- 2 onions, finely chopped
- 3 large stalks lemongrass, bashed
- 6 cardamom pods (I leave this out; biting into a cardamom pod is not for me)
- 1 piece pumpkin or a small squash, peeled and chopped into bite-sized chunks (about 1 kg)
- 250 ml vegetable stock

- 400 ml can reduced fat coconut milk
- 400 g can chickpeas, drained and rinsed
- Juice of 1 lime
- Large handful mint leaves
- Brown rice, to serve

Heat the oil in a sauté pan then gently fry the curry paste with the onions, lemongrass, cardamom, and mustard seed for 2–3 minutes until fragrant. Stir the pumpkin or squash into the pan and coat in the paste then pour in the stock and coconut milk. Bring everything to a simmer, add the chickpeas, and cook for a further 10 minutes until the pumpkin is tender. Serve warm, sprinkled with mint leaves, and add the lime juice, alongside a bowl of steamed brown rice. The curry can also be cooled and frozen for up to a month.

Puy Lentil and Coriander Pesto Bake with Sweet Potato Mash

Luckily, this one is easy to make. Everyone at home loves this. I always double up on the recipe. It's a simple bake that tastes even better on day two. Serve with a simple green salad.

- 2 medium carrots
- 150 g green beans
- 250 g potatoes
- 750 g sweet potatoes
- 400 g puy lentils
- 2 bay leaves
- Leaves from 6 sprigs of fresh thyme
- 2 teaspoons sea salt
- 1 teaspoon fresh ground black pepper
- 50 ml tamari

For the pesto:

- a good bunch of fresh coriander (approximately 50 g)
- 3 cloves of garlic
- 1 teaspoon sea salt
- 100 ml water
- 100 ml oil

Cut the carrots into bite-sized pieces. Trim the green beans and cut them in half. Cut the unpeeled potatoes and sweet potatoes into evenly sized pieces.

Rinse the lentils and put them into a large family-size pan with the carrots, bay leaves, thyme, salt, black pepper, tamari, and 1 litre of water. Turn the heat up high, and put the lid on the pan. Bring to the boil then reduce the heat, leave the lid ajar so the steam can evaporate, and simmer for a further 25 minutes, until the lentils are cooked and nearly all the liquid has gone. Finally, add the green beans.

Put the potatoes and sweet potatoes into a pan with enough water to cover. Bring to the boil, then reduce the heat and simmer for about 15 minutes, until tender.

Drain, put them back in the pan and mash. Season with salt and black pepper.

Preheat the oven to 200C/400F/gas mark 6.

Roughly chop the coriander and put into a blender with a peeled whole clove of garlic and other pesto ingredients. Blend until reasonably smooth.

Put the lentil mix into a baking dish and cover with the mash, spiking it up with a fork so you get crispy bits. Bake in the oven for 25 minutes. Serve with a generous dollop of pesto on each serving.

Spicy Lentil & Aubergine Pasta

Not my number one, but the kids devour it.

- 2 aubergines
- 1 red pepper
- 2 (400 g) cans of chopped tomatoes
- 1 tablespoon tomato puree
- 1 teaspoon chilli flakes
- 2 teaspoons paprika
- 3 teaspoons cumin seeds
- 3 teaspoons tamari
- 3 garlic cloves finely chopped
- 100 g puy lentils
- 2 teaspoons tahini
- 500 g brown rice pasta

Slice the aubergine and red pepper into small bite-sized pieces, and place them in a large saucepan with all the remaining ingredients, except the tahini and pasta. Pour in 350 ml of boiling water.

Place over a medium heat then return to the boil. Reduce the heat to a simmer, put on a lid, and cook for about 1 hour.

Stir in the tahini.

About 10 minutes before the lentils are ready, cook the pasta, drain, and stir into the aubergine sauce.

Vegetable Biryani

For a biryani, the rice and curry are first cooked separately, then together, for a final mingling of textures and flavours. You can take a shortcut by using a biryani curry powder instead of the individual spices and fresh chilli.

- 5 tablespoons coconut oil
- 1 bay leaf
- 3 cardamom pods, bashed (I leave this out; as I said in another recipe, biting into a cardamom pod is not for me)
- 1 teaspoon cumin seeds
- 5 large onions finely sliced
- 2 garlic cloves, crushed
- 2 teaspoons ginger, finely grated
- 1 large red chilli, finely chopped
- 1 teaspoon ground cumin
- 1 teaspoon ground coriander
- ½ teaspoon ground cinnamon
- About 250 g carrots, peeled and sliced into thin discs
- About 300 g potatoes, cut into cubes
- 200 g peas (fresh or frozen and defrosted)
- A generous squeeze of lemon juice
- 50 g sultanas
- 350 g basmati rice
- Large pinch of saffron
- Sea salt and freshly ground black pepper

To serve:

- 50 g slivered almonds
- Chopped coriander or mint

Heat 2 tablespoons of the oil in a large casserole over a medium-high heat. Add the bay leaf, cardamom pods, and cumin seeds and fry for a few minutes. Add 1 sliced onion and fry over a medium heat, stirring often, for about 15 minutes till golden and soft. Lower the heat and add the garlic, chilli, and ground spices. Cook, stirring for 2 minutes.

Add the carrots, potatoes, peas, and enough water to almost cover the vegetables. Bring to the boil then reduce to a simmer. Cover and cook, stirring from time to time, for 10–15 minutes. Season with salt and pepper and add a squeeze of lemon juice. Sprinkle the sultanas on top.

Meanwhile, rinse the rice thoroughly in several changes of water. Put into a saucepan with the saffron and a large pinch of salt. Add enough water to cover the rice by 2 cm. Bring to the boil then simmer very gently until the water is absorbed. Preheat the oven to 160C/ gas mark 3.

Cover the rice pan with a damp tea towel and a tight-fitting lid and turn the heat as low as possible. Cook for 5 minutes. Remove the lid and use a fork to separate the rice grains.

Spoon the rice in a thick layer over the curry in the casserole. Cover the pan with a damp tea towel and put the lid on tightly. Place over a high heat for a few minutes to get the curry bubbling again, then transfer to the oven for 20 minutes. Remove and leave to stand for 10 minutes.

When the biryani is cooking, heat the remaining 3 tablespoons oil in a large frying pan over a medium heat and add the rest of the sliced onions. Cook briskly, stirring often, for about 20 minutes until well browned. Season with salt.

Uncover the biryani and scatter over the browned onions, almonds, and coriander or mint.

Refried Beans Foldover

Savage.

This Mexican inspired foldover is a kind of burrito. It's particularly good with avocado inside.

- 2 tablespoons coconut oil
- 1 small onion, finely chopped
- 1 small garlic clove, chopped
- ½ red chilli, deseeded and chopped
- A pinch of dried oregano
- 1 large tomato, crushed, skin removed
- 400 g tin cannellini or borlotti beans, drained and rinsed
- Cayenne pepper or hot smoked paprika
- 3 freshly cooked soft flatbreads or pitta breads
- 2–3 tablespoons soured cream
- Sea salt and freshly ground black pepper

Toppings (optional):

- Grated goat's cheese
- Finely sliced red onion or chopped chives
- Chilli
- Sliced or diced avocado
- Cayenne pepper or hot smoked paprika

Heat the oil in a small frying pan over a medium heat. Add the onion and fry for about 10 minutes until soft, adding the garlic and chilli a few minutes before the end, along with the oregano.

Add the crushed tomato directly into the pan. Then let the mixture bubble and reduce for a few minutes. Add the beans and cook gently, crushing them down with a fork to make a coarse puree. Season well with salt and pepper, and add a pinch of cayenne or smoked paprika if you like spicy.

Put a spoonful of the mixture into the pitta with any optional extras.

Also good on tortilla chips.

Snacks

Chilli & Avocado Toast

- 1 ripe avocado
- Juice of 1 lime
- 1 teaspoon of olive oil
- 1 teaspoon chilli flakes
- salt & lots of pepper
- 2 slices of toast

Scoop the avocado flesh out of the skin and place in a shallow dish. Mash it with a fork until smooth. Stir in the lime juice and olive oil, chilli flakes, salt, and pepper.

Almond Butter & Banana

It's hard to stop eating this once you start.

- 1 ripe banana
- 1 tablespoon almond butter
- 2 slices of toast
- sprinkling of salt

Slice the banana then roughly mash in a bowl with a fork. Mix in the almond butter. Spread on toast and add salt.

Stuffed Savoury Chickpea Wraps

These are so good. Make them and stuff them with your favourite bits. When Fiona first made these, I wondered what I had done to deserve them.

These make a good alternative to sandwiches.

- 200 g gram flour
- 200 ml water
- ½ teaspoon ground turmeric
- ½ teaspoon ground cumin
- ½ teaspoon garam masala
- ½ teaspoon garlic powder
- melted coconut oil, for frying
- salt and pepper

To serve:

- Guacamole (Recipe in *Dips, Pestos, Dressings* section)
- Handful of fresh coriander
- Sprouted beans
- Pesto (Recipe in *Dips, Pestos, Dressings* section)

Combine the flour, water, spices, and some seasoning in a bowl. Whisk until smooth.

Leave the batter to rest for 5 minutes.

Heat a heavy pot over a medium heat and add a teaspoon of coconut oil.

When the oil is hot, turn the heat down and ladle a spoonful of batter into the pan, gently tilting in all directions to thin out evenly.

Cook for 4–6 minutes or until you can lift the edges with a fish slice to see the underside has turned golden brown. Flip and cook for a further couple of minutes. Lift onto a plate and cover with a clean tea towel to keep warm.

Serve with your favourite toppings.

Savoury Indian Pancakes

My favourite snack. Just the right texture and amount of spice.

This savoury Indian pancake is a spicy pan-fried bread made with fresh coriander, red onion, and Indian spices. It's very easy to make and tastes delicious. This is a vegan recipe and can be eaten as a snack or for any meal. I use gluten-free flour.

- Coconut oil, for frying
- ½ cup almond flour
- ½ cup tapioca flour
- 1 cup coconut milk, canned and full fat
- 1 teaspoon chilli powder
- ¼ teaspoon turmeric powder
- ¼ teaspoon freshly ground black pepper
- ¼ red onion, chopped
- 1 handful coriander leaves, chopped
- 1 chilli pepper, chopped
- ¼ inch ginger, grated

Mix almond flour, tapioca flour, coconut milk, and spices in a bowl until combined. Stir in the onion, coriander, chilli pepper, and ginger.

Heat a pan on a low-medium heat, add enough oil to heat the pan, then pour ¼ cup of batter into the pan. Spread the mixture out on the pan.

Fry for about 3–4 minutes per side. Cook until golden brown.

These do take a while to fry, so use a large pan so that you can make a few at a time.

Cumin-spiced Sweet Potato Wedges

These sweet potato chips make a great alternative to regular chips and are easy to make. Cut into wedges, toss with coconut oil, fresh lemon, and spices. Bake at a high temperature so they're lightly crispy on the outside and soft in the middle.

- 3 large sweet potatoes
- Juice of 1 lemon
- 3 tablespoons of coconut oil
- 2 tablespoons ground cumin
- 1 teaspoon ground coriander
- 1 teaspoon garlic powder
- Salt and pepper

Preheat the oven to 200C/fan 180C/gas mark 6.

Wash and scrub the potatoes. Cut each in half then cut each half into quarters so you have 8 chunky wedges from each potato.

Stir together the lemon juice and spices in a large mixing bowl. Add the potatoes and toss together, using your fingers to rub in the spices.

Arrange the potatoes skin-side down on a baking tray, and dollop the coconut oil into the tray. Bake in the oven for 30–40 minutes, tossing a few times, until soft on the inside and crispy on the outside.

Dips, Pestos, and Dressings

Brazil Nut Pesto

Brazil nuts are the very best natural source of selenium, an essential trace mineral required by the body. We need selenium for the normal functioning of our immune system and thyroid gland. Selenium can also help lower the risk of joint inflammation and plays a very important role both in terms of your body functioning properly and as part of your skincare regime.

- Handful of flat-leaf parsley
- 150 g Brazil nuts
- 1 clove garlic
- Juice of 1 lemon
- 2 tablespoons olive oil
- 1 tablespoon nutritional yeast
- Salt and pepper

Simply place all the ingredients in a food processor and blend for a couple of minutes to create a smooth, creamy pesto.

The addition of fresh lemon juice will help naturally preserve your pesto. Store in the fridge and use within 5–7 days.

Guacamole

Sometimes I eat so much of this I keep one eye on the door in case the guacamole police come to take me away.

One of the main skin benefits of eating avocados comes from their high oleic acid content. This monounsaturated fatty acid maintains moisture in the epidermal layer of your skin, helping it to keep soft and hydrated. An omega-9 fat, oleic acid is also involved in regenerating damaged skin cells and reducing facial redness and irritation. If you suffer from skin irritation and dryness, try eating more avocados for skin health and hydration.

- 3 ripe avocados, halved and stoned
- Juice of 1 lime
- Handful of fresh coriander, chopped, plus extra to garnish
- ½ red onion, finely chopped
- Pinch of salt

Use a spoon to scoop out the avocado flesh into a bowl. Add the lime juice, coriander, chopped red onion, and salt. Use the back of a fork to mash everything together.

Garnish with chopped coriander leaves.

Cambodian Wedding Dip

- (chilli and garlic paste can be used from a jar)
- 500 g chestnut or cup mushrooms or a combination
- 1 tablespoon coconut oil
- ½ small hot chilli, finely chopped
- 3 garlic cloves crushed
- 1 tablespoon curry powder or mild curry paste
- 2 tablespoons crunchy peanut butter
- 400 ml tin coconut milk
- juice of ½ lime
- a dash of soy sauce/tamari sauce
- finely chopped coriander (optional)

Finely dice the mushrooms.

Heat the oil in a large frying pan over a high heat. Add the mushrooms, and cook briskly, stirring often until all the liquid has evaporated. Add the chilli and garlic and cook for another minute.

Add the curry powder or paste and peanut butter, stir in thoroughly. Stir in the coconut milk. Let it bubble rapidly until thick, stirring occasionally so it doesn't burn. Add the lime juice and soy sauce to taste.

Serve warm or at room temperature with corn cakes or carrot and celery sticks.

Treats

Innocent Millionaire's Shortbread

I read a bit of advice once: "Don't eat anything bigger than your head." Very difficult when it comes to this recipe.

This is made with nuts, coconut oil, and raw cacao. Cacao is one of the world's best antioxidants.

For the shortbread base:

- 150 g ground almonds
- 75 g Brazil nuts
- 50 g pitted dates, chopped
- 3 tablespoons melted coconut oil (melt the coconut oil in a bowl over a pan of simmering water over a medium heat)

For the caramel layer:

- 100 ml coconut oil
- 3 heaped tablespoons almond butter
- generous pinch of salt
- 8 medjool dates, pitted
- 2 tablespoons maple syrup

For the chocolate layer:

- 100 ml coconut oil
- 4 heaped tablespoons raw cacao powder
- 2 tablespoons manuka honey

First make the base, combining all the ingredients in a food processor and blitzing until the mixture forms a chunky paste. Push the mixture into the base of a biscuit tray. Pop in the freezer.

Next make the caramel layer by combining all the ingredients together in a high-speed blender until you have a smooth gooey texture.

Spoon the thick caramel mixture over the cooled base and smooth out until even. Place in the freezer for an hour until hard.

For the chocolate layer, melt the coconut oil in a bowl over a pan of simmering water over a medium heat. Remove from the heat and stir in the raw cacao powder and manuka honey until the mixture is chocolatey and smooth. Pour this over the caramel layer and return to the freezer for 30 minutes.

Remove and cut into squares.

Store in the freezer and remove 30 minutes before serving to allow them to soften.

Avocado Chocolate Mousse Cake

I suggest you eat this with a well-disciplined partner to avoid overeating. If you must keep going, you could always eat each other.

A raw, sugar-free, dairy-free, egg-free dessert. It keeps for 5 days and also freezes well.

For the base:

- 300 g almonds
- 300 g cashew nuts
- 300 g pitted dates (medjool or regular)
- 2 tablespoons vanilla extract

For the topping:

- 4 ripe avocados
- ½ teaspoon salt
- 1 teaspoon cinnamon
- 4 tablespoons honey or agave syrup
- 90 g cocoa powder
- ¾ teaspoon vanilla extract
- zest of 2 oranges

To make the base, blend the nuts, dates, and vanilla extract together in a food processor until smooth and spread over the base of a 30 cm baking tin, compacting as you go.

To make the topping, put all the ingredients into a food processor or blender until smooth.

Spoon the chocolate mousse over the base, smoothing it out evenly, and leave to set in the fridge or freezer for 2 hours.

If you wish, decorated with berries before serving.

Granola Bars

Filling and delicious. I take them out with me.

- 50 g almonds
- 50 g cashew nuts
- 30 g sunflower seeds
- 100 g dried fruit
- 20 g goji berries
- 30 g desiccated coconut
- 40 g pumpkin seeds
- ¼ teaspoon salt
- 4 tablespoons coconut oil
- 60 ml honey
- 3 tablespoons 100% all-natural almond butter
- ½ teaspoon vanilla extract

Put the almonds, cashews, and sunflower seeds into a food processor and blitz until finely chopped. Cut the dried fruit into small pieces. Put the nut/seed mix and dried fruit mix into a bowl. Add the goji berries, desiccated coconut, and pumpkin seeds. Mix well. Add the salt.

Melt the coconut oil in a bowl over a pan of simmering water over a medium heat. Once melted, take it off the heat and add the honey, almond butter, and vanilla extract. Combine well using a fork.

Pour the wet ingredients on top of the dry ingredients and stir well to combine. Press the mixture into a tray lined with baking parchment.

Put into the fridge to set for 4 hours before slicing. Store in an airtight container in the fridge for up to 10 days, or freeze for up to a month.

Protein Grenades

Everyone at home loves these, so they never last long.

- 2 tablespoons crunchy peanut butter
- 1 tablespoon pea protein powder (Sunwarrior vegan protein, sprouted and fermented, is my favourite, but a little on the expensive side)
- 1 tablespoon ground linseeds
- 1 tablespoon desiccated coconut
- 1 tablespoon raw agave, honey, or maple syrup
- 1 tablespoon goji berries

Mush everything together in a bowl. Roll into mini balls, and sprinkle with coconut. Keep refrigerated.

APPENDIX B:

MY MARATHONS AND ULTRAMARATHONS

Rome Marathon, Italy, 21st March 2010
https://www.maratonadiroma.it/?lang=en

Dublin Marathon, Ireland, 25th October 2010
http://sseairtricitydublinmarathon.ie/enter-marathon/

Dublin Marathon, Ireland, 31st October 2011

Venice Marathon, Italy, 27th October 2013
http://www.huaweivenicemarathon.it/en/venicemarathon

Tralee International Marathon, Kerry, Ireland, 16th March 2014
http://www.traleemarathon.com/

Dublin Marathon, Ireland, 27th October 2014

Düsseldorf Marathon, Germany, 26th April 2015
https://www.metro-marathon.de/registration/marathon/

Cork City Marathon, Ireland, 1st June 2015
http://www.corkcitymarathon.ie/entry/

Düsseldorf Marathon, Germany, 24th April 2016

50km Forest Marathon, Portumna, Galway, Ireland, 11th June 2016
https://forestmarathon.wordpress.com/

Vienna City Marathon, Austria, 23rd April 2017
http://www.vienna-marathon.com/?lang=en

100km Forest Ultra, Portumna, Galway, Ireland, 10th June 2017

Last One Standing Ultra, Enniskillen, Fermanagh, Northern Ireland, 19th August 2017
https://www.atlasrunning.co.uk/last-one-standing

Armagh City Marathon, Northern Ireland, 26th August 2017
http://www.runarmagh.com/marathon/

Moscow Marathon, Russia, 24th September 2017
https://moscowmarathon.org/en/

Belfast to Dublin, 107 m Ultra, 30th March 2018
https://www.atlasrunning.co.uk

APPENDIX C:

MY BOOKSHELVES (AND OTHER FAVOURITES)

Books that changed the way I think about food

The Juice Master's Ultimate Fast Food by Jason Vale

The China Study by T. Colin Campbell & Thomas M. Campbell

Clean by Alejandro Junger

Whole by Howard Jacobson and T. Colin Campbell

Books that changed what I thought was possible

Born to Run by Christopher McDougall

The Road to Sparta by Dean Karnazes

Natural Born Heroes by Christopher McDougall

Eat & Run by Scott Jurek

Time to Fly! by Neil O'Brien

How to Get from Where You Are to Where You Want to Be by Jack Canfield

Iron War by Matt Fitzgerald

Run! by Dean Karnazes

Books that helped me train for marathons and taught me about endurance for ultras

Advanced Marathoning by Pete Pfitzinger & Scott Douglas

The Big Book of Endurance Training and Racing by Dr. Philip Maffetone

In Pursuit of Excellence by Terry Orlick

Thrive by Brendan Brazier

The Old Man and the Sea by Ernest Hemingway

An Unsung Hero, Tom Crean – Antarctic Survivor by Michael Smith

Books that gave me new ways to prepare food

Deliciously Ella Every Day by Ella Woodward

Radiant by Hanna Sillitoe

The Happy Pear by David & Stephen Flynn

The Kind Diet by Alicia Silverstone

What I listen to when I run

Half the time when running alone, I listen to something on my headphones. The rest of the time I just run and try to be in the moment, in the place, in my body. I have an ever-changing music playlist and a lot of podcasts I like. I listen to a fair bit of comedy. Other current favourites are Runner's World, Kevin Pollak, and The Minimalists. Next month this could be totally different!

My favourite gear

My watch is a Tomtom, and I love it. It tracks my distance, heart rate, route, and steps per minute. Plus, it has lots of training workout settings. I tend to put it on running mode, wait for GPS to pick up my location, and start. However, it is three years old and doesn't carry music, which means I have to carry my phone. Also, the battery time is only about 6 hours. Upgrade required shortly.

All my running shoes are "flats," which means the drop from heel to toe is minimal. I find minimal shoes equals minimal injuries. Short distances I run in Saucony, and all long distances in Hoka One One's. It took me a long time to learn I needed a slightly larger shoe for running. I lost many, many toenails before I figured it out. I found out by accident one day when I went to buy new shoes (in my favourite running shop Runzone in Rathgar, Dublin), and he didn't have my size. He recommended I try the larger pair. I haven't lost a toenail since, much to my wife's delight.

I tend to go for shorts with a skin-tight inner lining down my thigh (rather than the shorts with a net. I find the latter on a cold day freezes your b*llox off).

I have lots of T-shirts, many of them collected after a race. As a personal boost, sometimes I feel better in a shirt I've earned. However, on a wet day I go for skin-tight to prevent the material from cutting my nipples until they bleed. On a dry day, the choice makes less of an impact.

For long distance runs I wear 1,000 Mile double layer socks. They are the business for preventing blisters.

Documentaries I've enjoyed

Forks over Knives
Hungry for Change
Fat, Sick and Nearly Dead
In Defense of Food
Food, Inc.
Cowspiracy
Earthlings
What the Health

Many of the above are available on Netflix.

APPENDIX D:

MY TRAINING PLANS

A quick note before moving on to the training plans:

If you are new to training and have joined a gym, ask for help! Gyms can be very intimidating for a beginner. In the unlikely event that you were not offered help, ask an instructor for an assessment and a training plan. They are usually free and come with membership—but not always. Decide that you are worth it, and do not let yourself become one of the 80% who join a gym and pop in and out for the first month before dropping out never to be seen again. You are not here to tell your friends you are working out. You are here to better your life.

These training plans are basic and are for beginners. I have used many, but starting out I think these are the best. If you stick to them, they will work. You will finish your race in good health. If you are a seasoned runner, I would advise you to go online and find something more appropriate.

Sofa to 5k—beginners 8-week training plan
Half Marathon—beginners 12-week training plan
Marathon—beginners 18-week training plan

Sofa to 5k

Of all the training plans, this is the hardest. No question. When training for a marathon or half marathon, the chances are you have some level of fitness. That is not always the case with 5k. The first thing to do is get a buddy. Be accountable to each other. Stay positive, and try to be the best running partner you can be. Probably 90% of that will be showing up and not listening to excuses not to run.

If you are doing this alone, you need to be strong and determined. If you stick to your training plan, you could see some dramatic changes in your life. Before you make your plan, you must decide that you are doing the training regardless of the weather or how you feel. Your head will play tricks on you and tell you that you're too tired tonight, too hungry, too full, too hungover. Whatever the excuse, you must override the inner negative voice. There may, of course, be a time when you have a real reason, but know the difference.

Your Training Plan

If you can walk, you are ready.

This training plan has nothing to do with speed. It's about time on your feet. All you have to do is jog for a short period of time and then walk to recover then jog again, walk again, and repeat. You're going to jog/walk for 8 weeks, 3 times per week. This plan builds to a solid 40-minute run. Each jog/walk workout should start and finish with 5 minutes of easy walking as a warm-up and cool-down. The run segments should be completed at a relaxed effort (with minimal huffing and puffing). When in doubt, slow down, especially during the first 4 weeks and at the beginning of your workout for the second 4 weeks. Hold a brisk pace for each walk segment and repeat the run/walk pattern. Allow for roughly 40 minutes per session, building up to 50. This includes the warm-up and cool-down.

Week	Repeat 3 times per week	Duration
1	walk 1 minute – jog 30 seconds	30 minutes
2	walk 1 minute – jog 30 seconds	30 minutes
3	walk 1 minute – jog 45 seconds	30 minutes
4	walk 45 seconds – jog 45 seconds	35 minutes
5	walk 30 seconds – jog 60 seconds	35 minutes
6	walk 15 seconds – jog 90 seconds	40 minutes
7	jog for 30 minutes, walking only if/when required	
8	walk only when required	**5k**

Half Marathon

Before starting any training for running the 13.1-mile half marathon distance, whether it's in an organised race or on your own, you should be running regularly, approximately 10–15 miles per week. If you're not, you may not be ready to start. Jumping ahead tends to result in injury. Include hills in at least one run every other week or as regularly as you can.

Week	Mon.	Tue.	Wed.	Thu	Fri.	Sat.	Sun.
1	rest	2 miles	3 miles	3 miles	rest	3 miles	4 miles
2	rest	2 miles	4 miles	3 miles	rest	3 miles	4 miles
3	rest	2 miles	4 miles	3 miles	rest	3 miles	5 miles
4	rest	3 miles	5 miles	3 miles	rest	4 miles	6 miles

Reality check: Are you completing all your runs? When I first did this plan, there were six of us, and we celebrated every long run with brunch and coffee afterwards. We loved the progress and lived it.

Week	Mon.	Tue.	Wed.	Thu	Fri.	Sat.	Sun.
5	rest	4 miles	5 miles	4 miles	rest	3 miles	7 miles
6	rest	3 miles	4 miles	4 miles	rest	4 miles	8 miles
7	rest	4 miles	6 miles	4 miles	rest	4 miles	9 miles
8	rest	4 miles	6 miles	4 miles	rest	4 miles	10 miles

If you have completed the programme so far, you should be feeling good and fit by now. It is important to stick to the plan. Do not throw in extra miles or hills. Trust the plan. Do whatever it is you do to celebrate. The prize is the journey. The actual medal at the end of the race is just the cream.

Week	Mon.	Tue.	Wed.	Thu	Fri.	Sat.	Sun.
9	rest	4 miles	6 miles	4 miles	rest	3 miles	11 miles
10	rest	4 miles	5 miles	4 miles	rest	4 miles	12 miles
11	rest	3 miles	5 miles	4 miles	rest	3 miles	6 miles
12	rest	3 miles	5 miles	3 miles	rest	2 miles	13.1 miles!

Marathon

This beginner's marathon plan is designed so you finish your first marathon as healthy as when you started. As this is your first marathon, time is not an issue. It will be an experience—one you will probably never forget. It's important that you don't miss your long runs. You must also rest and eat sensibly to stay in good health. This plan is designed for anyone running less than 25 miles per week.

Week	Mon.	Tue.	Wed.	Thur.	Fri.	Sat.	Sun.
1	rest	3	3	3	rest	6	walk
2	rest	3	3[5]*	3	rest	7	walk
3	rest	3	4[6]	3	rest	5	walk
4	rest	3	4*	3	rest	9	walk

If you have been missing runs by this stage, maybe you are not ready yet. If you're keeping up with the schedule, your discipline should see you through. At this stage, rest is important on rest days and a good night's sleep will keep you from injury.

Week	Mon.	Tue.	Wed.	Thur.	Fri.	Sat.	Sun.
5	rest	3	5	3	rest	10	walk
6	rest	3	5*	3	rest	7	walk
7	rest	3	6	3	rest	12	walk
8	rest	3	6*	3	rest	13	walk

Hopefully, by now you're enjoying the training and how you feel after each session. You are now well on the way to being fit. Make sure to drink a lot of water the day before your long runs. Dehydration is the cause of many small and painful injuries.

Week	Mon.	Tue.	Wed.	Thur.	Fri.	Sat.	Sun.
9	rest	3	7	4	rest	10	walk
10	rest	3	7*	4	rest	14	walk
11	rest	4	8	4	rest	16	walk
12	rest	4	8*	5	rest	12	walk

---

5   Where Wednesday is marked with an asterisk, run every second mile fast.

6   If underlined, make it a hill run or take in as many hills as you can. Hills increase the strength in your legs.

This is the business end. Now you can start to visualise your race. Recovery drinks are important after every long run to repair your tired and torn muscles. Company is required for long runs. On your own, they can appear very long runs. Remember to enjoy the journey.

Week	Mon.	Tue.	Wed.	Thur.	Fri.	Sat.	Sun.
13	rest	4	9	5	rest	18	walk
14	rest	4	9*	5	rest	14	walk
15	rest	5	10	5	rest	20	walk
16	rest	5	8*	4	rest	12	walk

Nobody gets to this stage without having earned it. Sleep, rest, drink plenty of water, and eat well. Do not panic and try and fit in a long run in your last week. Trust the process. You are ready.

Week	Mon.	Tue.	Wed.	Thur.	Fri.	Sat.	Sun.
17	rest	4	6	3	rest	8	walk
18	rest	3	4	2	rest	rest	26.2

Long runs are the key; don't miss them. Take walking breaks anytime you need to. Replace the "walk" day with any form of exercise other than running if you wish.

On rest days, rest. Remember to enjoy your marathon; the hard work is done.

EPILOGUE
THE LONG ROAD

One out of four people in this country are mentally unbalanced.
Think of your three closest friends,
if they seem okay, then you're the one.

They say any race around a hundred miles won't kill you. But you might wish it had.

Two years ago, I read my first book on running by heart rate. The concept is quite simple. You keep your heart rate low, and you train using a heart rate monitor. Any time your heart rate increases over a certain figure, you slow down. Over time you get faster and stronger while keeping your heart rate within a certain limit. This method teaches you to burn body fat instead of sugar. The first step was to give up sugar and start running very slowly. After reading that first book, I decided within two years to run a 100-mile race. The time had come.

In preparation over the last two years, I had raced a 50k, a 50m, and a 100k along with several marathons. The next race up was the Belfast to Dublin ultra, (distance 107 miles). Nine years after I got up off my fat arse, I was finally mentally ready and running on heart rate, not sugar, fear, or anger.

The level of discipline and commitment, selfishness, and stubbornness required was matched by my first 5k when I started out. The first days of running were probably physically and mentally slightly harder. Then the desperation and pain didn't limit themselves to exercise. Now all pain is chosen and almost always worth it.

Most people won't come at exercise and well-being from anger. For those that do, good luck. Keep going.

For those that don't, good luck, keep going.

The journey may be different for a while, but it will collide, and the destination is the same.

There may be a wrong way to train,
but there is no wrong way to try.

Due to an injury, I had missed the first seven weeks of training. With only 10 weeks left I was toying with postponing the race. Unfortunately, I had been thinking about this for two years, and who knew what would be going on this time next year. I decided to go ahead. I didn't know if it was a good or a bad decision, but I certainly was not going to seek advice, in case I didn't like it.

For two of the last three weekends I had been snowed in. The other weekend I was smothered with a cold. Luck really hadn't been going my way on this one. On bank holiday Monday, with just twelve days to race day, I managed a 40-mile run. Weeks earlier I did a 28-mile run. This is nowhere near the number of long runs required to train for this race.

On the 40-mile I had mapped a ten-mile loop from my house. After every loop I had some soup and headed out again. On the 30-mile mark I was exhausted. I slumped down on the kitchen chair, and Fiona handed me a warm piece of toast with peanut butter, honey, and salt. I was hesitant to take solid food, but after the first bite, it was heavenly. My whole body was warming and tingling. I closed my eyes and got lost in the total physical pleasure of it. I really didn't know who was eating who.

At the end of the next 10 miles I was spent. Absolutely exhausted.

The thought of doing another 67 miles on top just seemed impossible. It was two days before I could walk without pain.

I was hoping I couldn't make it past 40 because I only set out to do 40. So on race day I hoped I'd make 107 miles because I would set out to run 107 miles. They say 90% of running an ultra is in your head … blah blah blah. That's what I was counting on.

The chatter in my mind went something like this:

Seven days to go. I will do 10 light miles today and maybe go for a walk with the dog. I'm going out for a few beers tonight. I will make those the last until the race is over.

Today I will draw up a list of ingredients for the week's food. I will arrive at the starting line next week well hydrated, well nourished, and ready as I can be.

My greatest fear is that I will stop and have to be picked off the roadside in some one-horse town on the outskirts of Dublin. The shame of not being made of the right stuff. What if I have a hollow core? Unless I'm injured, how will I look at myself again?

I could cancel. I could enter next year when I'm more prepared. But what if I'm dead next year? I know there are some fun zombie races, but I don't think any are for the actual dead.

Two days to go. The excitement is killing me.

For anyone who has not done anything outside of their comfort zone. I would highly recommend it. It's hard to know where the excitement ends and the fear begins.

My gut is a bit twisted. My insides are saying, "Are you for real? We have to process food and drink while you run for over 30 hours all going well?

We have to send oxygen to your muscles and keep you moving? Why? You're not the boss of me."

"Yes I am," I reply. *"Now please get on board. I can't do this without you."*

That's how it feels. Once we start running, I may have to concede that my gut is in control and is the big boss.

I know there will be pain, exhaustion, and fear—not necessarily in that order. If I come out the other side of this, I will be walking on air for a while.

Just to be on the starting line makes me proud of myself. To attempt such a race, with all the feelings and emotions that come with it, makes me feel very alive. A few people have asked me if I think it wise to attempt such a distance. I reply, "Yes."

My mother-in-law sent me a text message asking me not to make her daughter a widow.

BELFAST TO DUBLIN, 107 MILE ULTRA, 30TH MARCH 2018 (MY 16TH MARATHON)

It was a fresh morning in Belfast. I recognised a lot of runners from previous races. Lots of genuine smiles and nervous chats. There was a friendly, relaxed atmosphere.

Race end plus three days and I'm in my local village, Rathgar. I now have a new set of problems. I'm at the crossroads, it's lashing rain, and I'm carrying a cup of coffee. I'm on crutches. I can't figure out how to cross the road carrying the coffee. I feel like I'm in a "How did the fox, the rabbit, and the duck cross the river?" type situation, and I'm not the fox!

Today I get to sit and reflect on the race. I did it, and it feels good. Had I known beforehand what I would have to go through, I definitely would not have gone ahead. I know now that I am capable of enduring so much more suffering than I ever imagined. I suppose we all are. In a few days I would be back to normal. The only trace of this race would be the medal in my drawer and the etching on my soul.

The first 40 miles were tough, though enjoyable and very scenic. I don't remember a stretch that wasn't going up or down a mountain. We came out of Newry, and it felt good to be running towards the imaginary border between Northern Ireland and the Republic. I watched for the signs. The first confirmation was when the traffic speed signs changed from miles to kilometres. In my head I had broken the race into four parts: the North, darkness, daylight, and Dublin. We were now in part two, and everything was in working order. I was looking forward to the halfway point.

On Mile 45 the race took an unfortunate twist for me. My right foot started to blister. I felt it coming on for 10 miles, but I couldn't stop it. On Mile 47 my left foot started to blister. I had never had a blister before, ever. On Mile 60 I was suffering severe pain in both feet. Fiona temporarily patched me up. I was looking for the words to say, "I can't do this," when Fiona got into her car and drove off. She parked a mile up the road. When I got there, I could see the determination in her face and decided: *It's only pain, go to the next checkpoint and assess my feet then.* I knew that she knew that I would have difficulty with myself if I didn't finish and if there was even the slimmest of chances that I could have.

At the 70-mile checkpoint it was all pain. A medic dressed my feet as best she could. By this stage I could barely move without sharp pain. I had to make a decision. Call it a day, or carry on and finish. I weighed it up, and I decided the pain of the next thirty-seven miles would be less than the pain of not finishing. I had 14 hours before the cut-off time. I took the easy option, gritted my teeth, and moved on.

I'm now in awe of my crew. Fiona fed, watered, and bandaged me for 34 hours. Starting every 10 miles, then every 5 and for the last 37, every other mile. My son Jem spent 21 miles on the road with me when I was hurting and not the best company. My daughter Chris walked 2 of the last 3 miles with me. Without them I wouldn't have made it to Dublin. Without a caring crew, running this distance would not have been possible, not for me. I really don't know how anyone does it alone. Along the way, others joined me for support, or to see what madness looked like. Emma, Laura, Alfie and Alex, Dave, Aisling and Leo, you will never know the lift you gave when you walked with me that day.

My goal was to finish a 100-mile race. I learnt that if the plan doesn't work, change the plan, not the goal. My plan was to run the full distance. I had to change that plan and walk the last 37 miles. The last 37 miles was infinitely harder than the previous 70. With each step I could feel my blisters pinch, tear, burst, and bleed.

Eventually I turned the last corner onto Bridgefoot Street. I saw the finish line, sandwiched between the little Protestant church and Arthur's Pub. I had been picturing this moment for 10 hours now. I heard a big cheer. To my surprise, lots of friends had gathered, and we hugged like there was no tomorrow as I got my two medals. One for finishing and one for becoming a member of the 100-mile club. The feeling of finishing was intense. It was similar to the relief and joy of the birth of my first child.

Then into Arthur's for a beer.

WHAT RACES ARE NEXT ON THE RADAR?

Bergen, Norway

Toronto, Canada

Chicago, USA

Beirut, Lebanon

Prague, Czech Republic

St. Petersburg, Russia

Reykjavik, Iceland

THANK YOU FOR READING!

Thanks for reading all the way to the end of my book. Your time is valuable and much appreciated.

Want more?

Sign up on my blog at jcruns.com to be notified of any pending book releases or updated content.

Thank you so much for choosing to be on this journey with me, I'm so glad you stopped by.

Please don't hesitate to connect with me if you have any questions about this book, or if you just want to chat. I would be happy to hear from you, I enjoy connecting with readers.

Don't forget to sign up at jcruns.com.

Thanks again,

–Jonathan

A QUICK FAVOUR PLEASE?

Before you go can I ask you for a quick favour?

Would you please leave this book a review on Amazon?

It only takes a moment to go to Amazon and leave this book an honest review and help this book reach more readers.

Sign up on my blog page to be notified of any pending book releases or updated content jcruns.com

Please do not hesitate to connect with me if you have any questions about this book. I would be happy to hear from you.

Thanks again,

–Jonathan

ABOUT THE AUTHOR

Jonathan Cairns is a long-time runner who competes in marathons and ultra marathons around the world. If there's one thing he's learned, it's that running is more science than art. Feeding the body well, taking the right precautions against injury and honing the correct mindset are the only tools needed to build a lifelong running habit that sticks. *The Plant Based Runner: A Personal Guide to Running, Healthy Eating, and Discovering a New You* is dedicated to chronicling his journey and helping others replicate it. You can follow him at jcruns.com.

Follow me

Instagram @jc_plant_based_runner
Facebook @JCRuns

Made in the USA
Middletown, DE
31 May 2021